On Earth As It Is In Heaven

Whitney Nicholson

"On Earth As It Is In Heaven"
Copyright © 2020 by Whitney Nicholson

All rights reserved. No part of this publication may be reproduced, distributed, or transmitted in any form or by any means, without prior written permission.

Published by SpeakTruth Media Group LLC

www.speaktruthmedia.com

Book Layout © 2017 BookDesignTemplates.com Cover photo by Nick Verbelchuk

Cover design by Whitney Nicholson

Head shot by Wesley Mannino

ALL Scriptures in this book are taken from the KING JAMES VERSION: KING JAMES VERSION, public domain.

ISBN 978-1-7342646-2-3 (*pb*)

ISBN 978-1-7342646-3-0 (*eb*)

"On Earth As It Is In Heaven" / Whitney Nicholson. -- 1st ed.

Printed in the United States

www.wholelifestylemomma.com

To my best friend for life Kristopher,

Thank you for partnering with me to ensure that life runs smoothly while pursuing the calling God placed on my life. I couldn't do this without you. You're my rock, and I love you.

To my three beautiful children, Kaylee, Karter, and Kollin,

You inspire me, challenge me, and make me a better person every day. You taught me a love deeper than I ever knew existed. I love you munchkins.

To my parents,

Thank you for fighting daily to make me who I am through your prayers and encouragement. Thank you for the time you put into your grandchildren. You're a lifesaver to this busy, working mom.

Contents

Introduction 7

The Awakening 11

The Garden 28

Making Tent 48

Rise Up Levites 62

Judgment 75

Love 90

The Straight and Narrow 104

Spiritual Authority 152

Redemption 178

The Power of Praise 209

The Day of Harvest 230

Calling Down Heaven 250

A Letter to My Readers 271

About the Author 274

Introduction

My heart's desire for this book is that the message found in it will portray and express what the Father is trying to reveal about His true heart for people. I am learning His heart more and more every day, which has truly been a life-altering experience. I've been a Christian my entire life, but recently God has taken me into a deeper understanding of His love and His glory. Growing up, I was always close to Him, and I thought I was trusting Him through my faith. However, I have come to learn how genuinely shallow my knowledge of His love has been. I never realized how much I pushed away the things He wanted to show me in His heavenly realms.

Things are happening all around us that we cannot see. There are things we cannot explain. Honestly, the spiritual perspective of most people today is lacking. I know it was for me. They are afraid to even know about or tap into the potentiality of what those unseen things could mean or bring in our life. Human beings tend to be fearful of the unknown, often denying its existence. However, God is calling us to be aware of so much more than what we physically see around us. One of the reasons we fear the unknown is because we have never made it familiar to us. Neither do we know how to utilize nor operate in the power of the hidden realm of His glory. I believed in the existence of things in the spiritual realm, like angels and demons, but honestly, I really didn't want anything to do with them. I didn't want to see or feel them, even if they were considered "good." I just trusted that God was doing what He wanted to do with them. However, we have a huge role to fulfill in the heavenly realm. We can't have victory over the enemy if we are afraid to face him. When we see through God's perspective, our enemies are so much weaker than we perceived them to be initially. THEY ARE NOTHING compared to the goodness and power of God.

We are called to walk in faith and authority with what God has gifted us within this life. He has given us keys that will unlock the mysteries of the heavens and everything within it. The hidden realm is deeper than any two-dimensional concept that we can understand. When we get to know Christ, He gives us a spiritual, heavenly lens. What do I mean by "lens"? It is a perspective or how we see things. God will give you His lens, His perspective, to see how He sees everything. He shows us so we can learn what it is like beyond what we believe the world to be. We get to see His kingdom. When He allows us to enter those realms of His creation, we become familiar and comfortable with the unseen realm. We also begin to understand His intentions. We see peace. We understand how to conquer fear. We see how much bigger He is than anything that comes against us. We no longer blame the people around us, but what is actually influencing them from the spirit realm. Everything that we question is resolved when we operate within God's authority and grace.

This time right now is so holy to Him. He's trying to call us to attention, to show us the things we need to do to obtain an overflowing abundance of His goodness. He wants us to know; WE HAVE NOTHING TO FEAR. His presence is in us and working through us. All we have to do is recognize Him, accept Him, and learn how to live in and from His presence. When we do that, all of heaven will be reflected here on Earth. His perspective is so different from the things of this world.

Let's face it, we are coming up on some apocalyptic times. Here's the thing though, His definition of an apocalypse is so incredibly different than the world's perspective. The word "apocalypse" in Greek means an unveiling of revelation. To God, it means to see through His perspective. We tend to see destruction and the "end of the world" when we think of that word. However, He's trying to teach us not to operate from a skewed and tormented perspective of the world. He wants to unveil the "apocalypse" of reuniting heaven and Earth once again. He's calling for renewal. He's calling for an outpouring of goodness and removing the evil that torments His children. My heart is after the Father. He's shown me that He's not in it to bring wrath, but eternal life to His creation.

This book is for anyone seeking a deeper revelation of the Father's goodness, who hunger for an overwhelming outpouring of His incredible presence. He wants you to know that you are so loved and valued. You have such an important role in fulfilling in His kingdom. He will show you your position as a royal heir in His family. You are not called to suffer. You are a treasure and a champion. It's time for us to wake up and reject the lies we have believed. It's possible to reflect His kingdom here on Earth. Let's call heaven down to Earth together.

• CHAPTER 1 •

The Awakening

I was asleep and didn't even know it.

I have been a Christian for my entire life's existence, and it was only till recently that I have been awakened to heaven here on Earth. As I sit down to compile together everything within the last year that the Lord has shown me, I find myself in a struggle to even know where to begin. I have two giant notebooks filled with drawn-out detailed dreams and visions that He's given me. My mind has been dwelling on these things without rest for months. I never thought I would be the kind of person to have God-given dreams and visions.

I'm just a mom with many flaws. I thought only prophets and apostles experience these gifts.

The thing is, He wants to give everyone dreams and visions. All it took was me pursuing Him. The further I pursued, the more He showed me. And, I have to admit, I can't believe it took me so long to figure that out. Right now, more than ever, He is calling people to draw near to Him. He wants to show us how much we are loved. My faith and Christianity have been awakened. The funny thing is, I didn't know I was asleep. I am in such awe and utterly humbled that He considers me worthy enough to show me as much as He has so far. I was impacted so deeply that I sat down and asked, "God, okay, you gave me all this, now what"?? I guess you could say, this book was His answer. I want you to feel even a smidgen of what He's made me feel recently. I have been forever changed and my heart is for you to feel a hope greater than anything in this world, because there is hope for everyone.

Before these recent revelations, I came to a point in my faith where I was seeking a deeper-rooted existence. I kept being drawn to the word TRUTH. That's all I kept hearing for the longest time. The truth was missing in so many aspects of daily life. Maybe, it's because we live in a time and culture where there's a concerted effort to manipulate us into believing an agenda that is far from the real truth. I think people desire authenticity. They want the genuine, raw truth. And I do too. We're tired of being entangled in a web of lies and manipulation. I was determined to dive deeper. I wanted to help people. I needed help myself.

Regarding the things that God was revealing to me, I read close to a hundred books, listened to every available podcast, watched all the relevant YouTube videos I could get my hands on, all within a year. I continued to see and hear the same theme from the people around me. I noticed their sense of hopelessness and emptiness. My heart grieved for those struggling. There's so much societal pressure on people, which causes them to drift away from a more profound connection of identity and worth for themselves and others around them. There is a significant disconnect. I felt like I was watching people who were stuck on a vicious and toxic hamster wheel of life, not knowing how to get off. And, honestly, it was easy to recognize because I started to feel the same way.

As I read all the self-help material out there, I felt like something was still not right. It all felt so shallow. The world is full of so much "self-help" advice these days. Human beings are not the Savior of anything. Where I was going wrong was that I was focusing on the things that I was capable of doing instead of what God was capable of doing. You can quickly get raveled up in an "all about me and my ambitions" type of mentality. The ability to help yourself is wonderful, and I'm a huge advocate for it, but the problem lies in the fact that you go to yourself first. That's exactly what I was finding myself getting caught up in.

Instead of bringing my concerns and questions to God first, I would think "Ok, what do I need to do"? I didn't rest my trust in Him to provide the answers. I thought I was leading a life like that, but my self-driven and motivated mentality drifted me further away from God. My ambitions became a distraction from the truth and what mattered most. I had to redefine what the truth is in my life. We hear that Jesus is the truth and the way, but so often we don't live by it. We have no issues with quoting that though. We all get caught in that at some point in our lives. Key is, you have to recognize it and catch it before your life spirals out of control. I had to bring it back to Him. He had to be my focus again. The moment I gave into that realization and acted on it by making time for Him again, like desperately seeking Him and letting myself go, that's when things started really happening. As a result, my life became LIFE-giving.

I've always felt God. I knew His voice, but I needed to stop treating Him like a cousin, and more like my best friend. Even more than that, I needed to get to know Him better than I knew myself. I needed intimacy with the Father more than ever before. As I made myself known to Him, the more He made Himself known to me. If I felt off and incomplete, I had to take it to Him. The world is filled with so many "truths," but worldly truths do not come with a plan. They do not come with a hope. I had to turn to Jesus. I had to take it to Him in every moment I questioned. I couldn't wait till He was the last option. He had to be my first option. My first thought had to be, "what does God want me to do"? As soon as I started to do that in each moment, my life changed. I mean that with every bone in my body. You need to know though; it takes practice and I'm not always perfect at the practicing part. However, He's so patient. He understands the flaws in humans. He sees our heart when we finally do realize that we need to take it to Him first. He proved His patience with me when He spoke in a way that He had never spoken before. He started giving me dreams. He gave me the answer to my search for, yes you guessed it, TRUTH.

I remember in the very first dream that I had this year, I was reading a book and I came across a word that I couldn't pronounce. However, I somehow knew that it was a Hebrew word. It was blurry, but I could see that it started with a "T" and also had an "i" in it as well. I didn't know what it was, but I heard a voice say "Titus." The word that I read in the dream wasn't Titus though. When I woke up later "Titus" was the first thing that came to mind. I was so anxious to know why I had such a specific dream, so I opened the Bible up to the book of Titus to see if something sparked. I knew if I would see the word again, I would immediately recognize it. The whole book of Titus has to do with seeking Jesus and looking for His return. I then got to one of the last paragraphs of the book and then my jaw dropped. I saw the word Tychicus. There it was! That was the word I saw in my dream! I immediately got chills from head to toe. Who or what is Tychicus? I'd never heard of this, much less seen it in the Bible. God told me right then, "be a Tychicus." I'm like, "okay I hear you, but who is this guy"? I studied further. Prepare yourself for this one. Tychicus was a faithful fellow servant of Paul's. Paul was the author of the majority of the New Testament and his mission was to speak to the churches about Jesus, His love, His TRUTH, and His return. His mission was to have a "heaven reflected on Earth" encounter.

Tychicus was a highly favored friend of Paul's. He was mentioned a few times in the New Testament. He was an encourager. In Colossians 4:7 Paul says, "All my state shall Tychicus declare unto you, who is a beloved brother, and a faithful minister and fellow servant in the Lord." Next verse says, "whom I have sent to comfort your hearts." As I tried to find other mentions of Tychicus, I looked at the mission of Paul a little further. Then I saw the very first verse in Titus, "Paul, a servant of God, and an apostle of Jesus Christ, according to the faith of God's elect, and the acknowledging of the truth which is after godliness." There it was, TRUTH. Paul left the assignment of speaking TRUTH to Tychicus. WHOA. Okay God, I'm listening.

Because of the foundation I had within my faith, I knew what I had to do. If I wanted to find truth, I had to go right to the source, Jesus. John 14:6, "I am the way, the truth, and the life." That had to be my first step. I had to teach myself to seek Him first, no matter what. I had to go beyond just saying it. My whole life I was told to "seek and you shall find." I heard that Scripture repeated over and over. I thought I understood it, but I did not. So often, we find ourselves frustrated when we don't have the answers. We get angry about the things we don't understand. Questions like, "Why the heck does evil exist," and "why do bad things happen to good people"? We feel confident and secure, until something bad happens right? I had so many unanswered questions. By faith, I knew God was there because of various times He had proven Himself to me. But how do I begin to understand anything beyond that? How do I comfort those who are frustrated and suffering as well?

In these situations, faith, trust, and humility must be put into practice. Three key ingredients to the Holy Spirit gumbo. (Sorry, my Louisiana is showing through, ha!) Anyway, I quickly learned that all Jesus requires of us is to go to Him first. That's it, Jesus first! So how do we do that? If we believe that He exists, which is what we call our faith, we can build a relationship with Him. Relationships are established as we get to know someone. We intentionally make time to spend with the person, which is how we start. We make the time. The more time you spend with the person, the deeper you get to know them. You understand them. They reveal themselves to you. They let you into their thoughts. You learn their desires. Getting to know someone creates a bond of trust. Because we understand their intentions, we can see why certain actions may or may not take place right? It's the same with getting to know God.

We focus much of our time on the things that only appear right in front of us. We are like mules with blinders. We get frustrated when we don't see or understand things. It holds us back and we start to let our doubt take over. When that happens, our trust in God slowly fades. I had to fight my thoughts. I still must fight my thoughts. I had to stop asking why and hand Him my worry. I had to train myself on how to put aside the questions and learn to wait on Him. How do you wait? You thank Him BEFORE you get the answer knowing that the answer will come. You throw on your favorite praise music and you sing your worry and doubt away. You write out and memorize powerful Scriptures that strike your soul and you declare them out loud over your life. The moment you get in that habit, He gives you the answers. He even shows you why you might not have gotten the answers you thought you should have. He shows you that it was all for your good and for your protection. Think of protecting a child. Their comprehension is limited. As a parent, we protect them by taking things away (like social media from someone who is way too young). We know the consequences of what could happen if given to someone who isn't ready to handle or understand it. We do it for their protection because we love them. They might get angry, but it's because they weren't quite ready to handle the truth.

Sometimes God handles things with us the same way. At some point in our life, hopefully, sooner than later, we recognize we don't know everything. For some of us, that might be a hard pill to swallow. Culture is continuously evolving in front of us, and sometimes, what we thought we knew could very possibly be wrong. Perhaps we couldn't see the whole picture. There was a deeper meaning behind what was laid out right in front of us. Sometimes we don't get answers from God for our protection. Other times it might be we simply did not pursue the truth through Him. The Scripture clearly states, "seek and you shall find." SEEK AND YOU SHALL FIND. All my life I was misusing what this means. Without realizing, I was seeking or asking ONE time thinking that because He was powerful and can do all, He was going to answer me. That's not how God always operates. He wants us to grow and be loved in ways beyond what we could imagine for ourselves. He doesn't hold back in any way. Sometimes the best comes with a process. It comes with a relationship. Going deeper with Him creates room for deeper understanding. I'm not always ready to get answers when I think I am. I'm clueless and I have to remind myself I need God. God is limitless. I am limited. He won't put us in a box when it comes to our growth. He sees us at the highest value, and He holds us there. It's us who limit ourselves. Think about it; if we get a quick answer, we may not appreciate the depth and value of what we have received. What does that mean? When I mention "peeling back layers," I'm talking about the struggles in our life. These moments are opportunities to cling to God and allow Him to remove the sin and unbelief from our lives. If we refuse to go through the process, we will miss the things He intended for our benefit. We have to get out of our comfort zones to experience the more of Him that He wants to give us through relationship.

I'm not saying God gives us struggles, that might be our viewpoint on how we see it. Struggles come because we live in a fallen world. Remember, in the beginning, what God created was perfect. Imperfection came in when Adam and Eve ate the forbidden fruit in the Garden. Sometimes things are revealed to us in unexpected ways, and we tend not to like it. We view it as harder because it wasn't what we expected or prepared ourselves to experience. Honestly, many times, our struggles are a direct result of ignoring His direction. If I don't understand something or if I lose trust in Him, the responsibility falls on me. I have to ask the question; did I spend enough time getting to know Him?

1 John 3:22 reiterates the previously mentioned Scripture with a little more detail, "Whatever we ask, we receive of Him, because we keep His commandments, and do those things that are pleasing in His sight." Before, due to my own tunnel vision of selfishness, I failed to notice the "because

we keep His commandments" part. I expected Him to just give me what I asked of Him because I loved Him. That is what we tend to think right? The thing is, I was taking advantage of Him and I didn't even know it. I wouldn't fully submit to Him. I wasn't approaching Him with a full repentant heart. I had to approach Him with reverence. His presence deserves a clean and pure heart. He knows I mess up, but He wants me to recognize it and try to do better. He doesn't want me to live in shame every time I make a mistake. It's quite the opposite. In order to take away sin and shame, you have to acknowledge it, repent, and give it to God. He can't take away what I don't offer up to Him. He can't give me the good in Him if I can't get rid of the bad that is happening in me. He wants to dwell in me and become close with me because He wants to see me succeed. But He does not force Himself on me. He wants me to allow Him to give me His good. He's really such a gentle and sweet Father.

When we genuinely seek Him first, He becomes our inner voice. His Holy Spirit inside of us gives us peace. We learn His will. How do we learn His will? What is His will? I like to think of God's will as His character and intentions. His will is also discovered in His Word. When you spend time reading His Word and humble yourself by approaching Him with a repentant and grateful heart and mind, He will let you know more about who He is. He explains the things you don't understand. You'll know when He does it too. For me, He did that by giving me dreams and visions.

I have always heard of people who had the blessings of God given dreams, seeing visions, even hearing His voice audibly. I thought that was something specific to them, I guess. Was I jealous? Sure. I wanted those gifts but didn't know how to obtain them. I've felt His presence but didn't know how real He could make Himself to me until I was intentional about pursuing Him. I'm not talking about here and there either. It couldn't just be five-minute prayers in my car on my way to work anymore. I needed to give Him more. At first, you don't see how you can even make more time when you're a busy working mom of three. Honestly, that was an excuse I kept giving myself to justify my actions or lack thereof. The truth is you make time for the things you love. I had to look at where my time was going and where I spent most of my time. I had to come to understand that whatever I gave my time to, that's what I made a priority in my life.

You get a hard reality check when you make yourself aware of that.

Once I genuinely took the time to pursue Him, without any expectations, nothing other than to just get to know Him, that's when my awakening happened. I had to stop going to Him expecting something in return. Always going to Him asking for things. I had to first love Him; love Him "because He first loved us." Think about your own relationships with other people. Wouldn't you be more inclined to pour into them when they genuinely approach you just to love you, expecting nothing in return? That's when you feel loved, not used for someone else's advantage. That's how it is with Him. God deserves more.

Then it happened, I had a dream. Ha! Maybe that's how it happened with Dr. King too! I then had another dream and another. Then I started to see visions of things even when I was awake. I would hear clear as day voices speaking to me in my dreams. How do I know it was from God? Because there is no way, I would have ever been able to come up with all these things on my own. Things that I would dream I would hear later that day on a podcast. I would search for something online, and what I saw in my dream would appear out of nowhere precisely in detail. I would search the Bible about the things I saw in my dreams to see what Scripture had to say about it, and sure enough, it would be there almost word for word. Scriptures I never knew existed. At first, it sort of freaked me out, but He manifested Himself to me straight from the unseen spiritual realm and took me right into the natural or seen places. The more He would give me, the more I would obsessively spend time reading His Word. God was removing the blanket I had put over my head, a covering that blinded me and kept me from Him.

Here's the thing I realized, if you haven't found the answer, you haven't been seeking long enough. You seek it, TILL you find it. You pursue Him, TILL you find Him. Don't limit God by limiting your time spent with Him. If you haven't heard or felt Him, did you stop pursuing? I have never felt such a tangible sense of completion in all my life. Yes, an actual, physical feeling of something caused by the unseen realm. For the first time in my life I have such clarity about what it means to feel and be alive. All I can explain is that I have been awakened from my sleep.

That's the reason He asked me to write this book. He wants me to let you know that He loves you. He wants you to feel that tangible, deep value of worth He holds for you. He's calling you to open your eyes to Him. This closeness of His Holy Spirit isn't just meant for Abraham, Moses, or King David. It is intended for us all. We're the ones who create the separation when we ignore Him. He's right there, waiting. He loved us first. All we have to do is love Him right back. Jesus first! Remember, He is the Way, the Truth, and the Life, no one goes to the Father except through faith in Jesus Christ.

• CHAPTER 2 •

The Garden

After I had that first dream, I started my truth journey by reading Genesis. Honestly, I can't remember what led me to begin with Genesis in the first place. Nevertheless, that's where it started for me. How appropriate, "genesis" means "in the beginning." Soon enough, I started ripping apart and studying Scripture. I would research the original Hebrew text and paid close attention to verbs and even articles within the wording. If I didn't understand a word or what it meant, I would look at where it was mentioned elsewhere in the Bible to grasp a more significant meaning. In doing that, I began to uncover a whole world full of mysteries. I call it "the unveiling of the Scripture" like a 7-layer dip. It isn't called the living Word for no reason. Each time you read it; He shows you something new. It's because each Scripture has deeper meanings like layers. The way you view it one time may mean something deeper the next. It doesn't disprove the first but expands on it, which is one thing to ALWAYS keep in mind. Scripture NEVER contradicts itself. And God NEVER changes. He is bound to and by His Word. If the Word seems to contradict itself to you, it means you misunderstand its context, or you are not considering the totality of Scripture. You can uncover what it means by studying where it may be mentioned elsewhere in the Bible to grasp a common theme, which is a great way to back up your interpretations. It is also important to understand who that particular part of Scripture is written to, and it's time and place, and what's called a dispensation. I also strive to learn more about God's intentions behind the Scriptures. It helps me to learn His character.

God is very cyclical too. You often see repeated themes. He does that for a reason. Everything and I mean EVERYTHING that is in the Bible has a purpose. Yes, even the boring lineage lists. I'll give you an example, take Luke

Chapter Three. It goes through an incredibly long list of the lineage of Jesus. Why, you ask? Well, there's always a reason. We just have to be looking for it. I counted how many fathers and sons were mentioned on that long list of names. Seventy-seven names were listed. Jesus was first in the list, and God was seventy-seventh. If you didn't know this already, numbers are very significant in the Hebrew language. Each letter of the Hebrew alphabet represents a number. The number "7" represents God. "G," even in our alphabet, is the seventh letter. Things and people in the Bible were always renewed and sanctified on the 7th day. The Sabbath, the holy day, was the seventh day. I could go on and on. Well, God within that lineage list was number seventy-seven. We know that Jesus is God, and He was number "1" on the list. As Scriptures note, He is the First and the Last, the Beginning and the End, the Author and the Finisher. No matter which way you count from that list, you still start and end with Him. He does that type of thing over and over throughout the Bible to blow your mind. When you begin to see these things, you quickly realize how infinite God is in everything He does.

I've come to learn that the Bible is a book full of exciting and mind-blowing mysteries that I never knew existed. It's also the world's #1 best-selling book of all time, and it's full of historical accounts for multiple millennia. The more advanced we are getting with our discoveries of science and ancient archeology, the more and more they keep proving everything Scriptures have told us. Nothing is full of mystery as much as the Old Testament. Never would I have ever thought the Old Testament would have grabbed my attention more than the New Testament. Genesis is one of the best examples.

Genesis confirms everything originated in the Garden. The foundation of all that we have come to know and understand came from the Garden. Although that may seem like the most obvious statement, maybe I can share a teensy bit of the revelations He has shown me.

Often, we have a shallow concept of creation, like the Tree of Life, the Tree of the Knowledge of Good and Evil, or the consequence of eating forbidden fruit, and so on. Mysteries are hidden within the verses. Like why did the Tree of the Knowledge of Good and Evil exist in the first place? Why did God tell them not to eat the fruit, and why the heck would the serpent's seed have hostility toward the woman's seed only by eating a piece of fruit? I've come to learn that when something is odd, it's usually significant.

For months, I missed the key elements. I didn't understand certain things, but I trusted God in knowing that it was for a reason, and it was for our good. You must believe it and choose to look through the lens of His goodness. It is so important because it's His truth—the absolute truth. All it took was me trusting. Just because I may not see or understand it at first, doesn't mean it's not there. Modern science often quotes The Reverend William Wright in saying, "Absence of evidence does not mean evidence of absence." If God is there, He is working for my good. I have to search and study what God is saying and doing just like Scriptures tell me to do. 2 Timothy 2:15, "Study to show thyself approved unto God, a workman that needeth not to be ashamed, rightly dividing the word of truth."

So, before I go into the Tree of the Knowledge of Good and Evil, let me first start with how I believe God intended our existence to be in the Garden. First, with The Tree of Life, this wasn't just any old tree haphazardly planted in the Garden. The Tree of Life placed in the center of the Garden represented the God kind of life and the unification of heaven and Earth. It's such a powerful concept and it's something that He wants us to have access to when we become one with Him. He can still bring us back to the Garden, back to His secret place of protection with Him. To me, it represented the presence of God and life given to man through it. He created us to have life with Him. It's reflected even in our physical being.

Trees are significant in the Bible. We are called trees of righteousness, and there's a good reason. It's no coincidence that much of our bodies' cellular makeup look like trees either. Look up images of the following: lung branches, nerve trees, blood vessels, the brain, and its stem, and coolest of all, the placenta. The blood vessels inside literally look like an upright tree. The placenta is such a beautiful representation of the Tree of Life.

He recently showed me a vision of a cell that contained a bright center. There were active waves all around the cell. The waves looked similar to the grooves of a brain. They branched out further and further, making it appear like a tree. Heck, maybe that's how the Tree of Life looked, who knows? God's handiwork is displayed in many forms. I also believe the fruits of the Spirit are the fruits produced on the Tree of Life. You know love, joy, peace, patience, gentleness, goodness, faithfulness, meekness, and self-control. Each represents the character of God and His Spirit that establishes the God-kind of life in man. When we become one with Him, we take on those characteristics. We take part in communion with Him and His presence, the Tree of Life. The Bible says that the Tree of Life was in the midst of the Garden of Eden. It represents that He is the center of all things, the bright nucleus within the universe and within us.

The Tree of Life represented everlasting natural and spiritual life. It was a representation of God in a "tree" form. It always brought forth the perspective of life. The Bible's tree theme is vast. You can study that more in-depth later to find out for yourself. Wood, rods, branches, and trees are all symbolic of giving life to and the protection of man. The rod, for example, was a wooden tool used by a shepherd to keep his sheep from harm. It was used to prevent them from falling off a cliff as well as fighting off predators. We see the blessing of wooden implements in Psalms 23:4, "Thy rod and thy staff comfort me."

Trees are also compared to people and the life they represent throughout Scripture. Mark 8:24 says, "And he looked up, and said, I see men as trees, walking." Genesis 49:22, "Joseph is a fruitful vine even a fruitful vine by a well; whose branches run over the wall." The tree could also be symbolic of the pathway to God. It is also a confirmation that we are made in God's image. He is the Tree of Life; we are created with repeating symbols in our bodies of trees. Joseph's hypothetical "tree" gave life to others through resources that came directly from the kingdom of heaven. Our existence is to be filled with life and to, like a branch, give life out to others so they can find His kingdom through Christ as well.

Before Eve and Adam chose to ignore the commands of God, causing the curse to enter the picture, God was walking amongst them. He was one with Adam and Eve. He didn't exalt Himself above them; He allowed them to be one with Him. In a way, He allowed them to be god-like because He gave them access to His thoughts and ways. The Tree of Life and the free access to it was what unified heaven to Earth. I believe God's original intention was for us to reign with Him as one.

Now comes the Tree of the Knowledge of Good and Evil. I wrestled with this one for so long, and to some extent, I still don't COMPLETELY understand it. However, I feel like God gave me more clarity, peace, and understanding. So, here's my question to God. Why even have this tree in the Garden, right? Here's the deal, I think God intended the tree to be for Him and His responsibility. He knew the knowledge would hurt us, so staying away from the fruit was for our protection. His directive, "you must not eat the fruit," also became representative of our free-will ability to choose Him and obey. When He created man, He wanted to give him the option to freely choose. He doesn't force Himself on His humanity. Although, He put eternity in the hearts of men (Eccl. 3:11). It was the man's choice to ignore the advice of His Father. However, once man chose to disobey, God used their sin to turn it for His good. He made it into something that would help man see His glory even greater. He uses our mistakes to help us grow if we are willing.

The knowledge of the world, and the order in which it works, is a great responsibility to bear. No man can fully comprehend it; only God who created the Universe. It's so complicated and intricate. His intention, when He designed us, was for our lives to be simple. It could have been and still could be if we learn to see through His eyes. We lost a perfect existence when Adam and Eve looked through another lens. God wasn't trying to deprive His creation of knowledge. He was trying to teach them how to honor His Word and see through His lens only, the one that brings life. God knew how everything functioned; He created the order. He knew the actions and the counteractions of the world's existence. For something to evolve into something better, there has to be an opposite counterpart to cause it to become stronger. You see, God had a creation process and a plan.

In science, for an action to happen, you must have a counteraction. For instance, when a person blows air out into a balloon to expand it, the lungs contract. How does this relate to creation? When He formed creation's molecules and nanoparticles, a counterpart makes the other react. For example, the gravity force of what we call "space" causes a reaction of protons leading to the creation of a molecule. The force was the counteraction of the proton. For every force, there is an opposite or opposing force that causes action. In God's perfect original creation, there was no counterpart considered evil. Everything had a purpose and a function for benefit and blessing. The choice to disobey God removed His protective covering over Adam and Eve. It caused them to have a cursed outlook on themselves and the environment around them. There was now an opposing force counteracting God. Evil now gave them the definition of good. They didn't know there was a difference beforehand. The perspective lens of God and choosing to obey His voice, allows us to see the world through His eyes and the perfection within it. Anything that is outside of God's perspective does not bring life. That's why He urges us to draw near to Him, receive Christ as Lord so that we will have abundant life and be able to view life through His perfect perception again.

God knows everything, which is why He is called "Omniscient." He knows the counteraction to what is good. He can handle the knowledge of what's opposite without causing harm. He can look at both functions as purposeful without messing up and perverting it. We don't know how to do that without His lens and His help. Satan manipulated our perception and continues to bring harm within the counteraction. He was the originator of the cursed opposite force with his own decision not to choose God. Satan creates a counterfeit of what God creates. He creates a false peace of God's shalom. He perverts God's agape love into a sadistic lust. The symbolism of Lucifer's fall was within that Tree of the Knowledge of Good and Evil. God was protecting Adam and Eve from the knowledge of Satan's ways by telling them not to partake of the fruit of that tree.

Here's where it got messed up. While Adam and Eve were enjoying the fruit of the other trees fine, the spirit of Satan manifested through the notorious serpent that hung out on the tree God told them not to eat from its fruit. To me, that tree represented Satan's kingdom. I feel that maybe that tree came about when Lucifer decided to turn from God. He wanted to create his own kingdom. You see, Satan was jealous that man now had dominion over creation and how close they were with God. Before Lucifer fell from heaven, before man was created, he held high power and status. He also had tremendous knowledge of how everything worked. Heck, perhaps God created the Tree of the Knowledge of Good and Evil as a reminder and symbol of Lucifer's pride and rebellion against God. He, Satan, is the one who established the counterforce of evil. Eating the fruit of this tree would corrupt the vision we have of the Kingdom of God and the Tree of Life.

Lucifer's pride destroyed his bond with God. He wanted to exalt himself ABOVE God instead of walking WITH Him. God gave Adam and Eve the freedom to choose because it's not true love without that liberty. Even so, they could CHOOSE to ignore the voice of God. The serpent understood the free will they were given. Deception took place when Satan caused Eve to give in to the desires of the flesh. Meaning, he convinced her to put herself above the will and good intentions of God, just like he had. He persuaded her to pursue knowledge and power first, over God. She didn't fully understand what was happening, and the serpent used that to deceive her into thinking she lacked something. He said, "You will become god-like." If you read Genesis 2:6, her perception of the tree changed. It's like Satan made her see a different tree. You know why? The moment you allow your flesh to decide how to focus, it changes your perspective. You put a cover, or veil, like the Bible calls it, over your head, which blinds you from God's good and perfect will for us.

Think about it. Adam and Eve had everything they needed. They walked WITH God, not below Him. Satan, which means adversary, wanted to divide Adam and Eve from God. Through his tactics, he deluded them into believing they lacked something when they did not. The moment they ate the fruit, they ignored the voice of the Father. The Scriptures say, "Their eyes were opened." The "cursed seed" became the cursed perspective that corrupted their soul. They became unclean. It wasn't God Who created the separation after the sin; it was the choice of ignoring Him. Sin separates us from God; He is perfect and clean. You can't mix the unclean with the clean. It's not because He doesn't love and doesn't want to be with us, it's because you can't corrupt the clean. God created man perfect like Him, with no flaws, fears, or a cursed perspective. The sin of rebellion corrupted their makeup both spiritually and physically and because of this, the cursed flesh had to be separated. If God allowed the two to mix, it would alter the makeup of the form. I'll explain how in a second.

When Adam and Eve were partaking of the things of God by obeying His Word, they were considered "living" beings. That's why Adam didn't name Eve, which means "mother of the living," until AFTER they sinned. The reason is that he didn't know there was an alternative until he was made aware of it after partaking of the knowledge of good and evil. The flesh became cursed both in the spiritual sense and in the natural. Whatever happens in the spirit is reflected in the natural, remember that. "Thy will be done on Earth as it is in heaven" (Matt. 6:10). The moment they listened to the adversary, they separated themselves from God. They corrupted their spirit. It was no longer perfect, so they took on the seed of Satan which was the corrupted perspective and the fear that damaged their physical being. When God created the fruit of the trees, He mentions the seed is "within itself." The moment they took in evil, the seed of evil entered, the seed of corruption. That's why He says there will be hostility between your seed (Satan) and her seed (God's seed). Until God's ultimate will is complete (when the power of sin is no more), there will always be the duality between good and evil. The evil is combatting the good. The only way to overcome it is through our faith and hope in Jesus.

So how did sin corrupt the natural body that will ultimately cause death? Let me explain. Since I'm a nurse and have studied science, it came in handy when He revealed this to me. When Eve thought she lacked something, then Adam too, fear set in bringing pressure and stress on them. Their eyes were opened; they noticed their nakedness. They felt exposed. What happens to you when you feel exposed? Your flesh becomes the focus, and you feel small, vulnerable, and unprotected. They suddenly feared God as well. Their choice to listen to the desires of the flesh made them cover themselves from God.

What happens to our cells when we feel pressure and stress? Our body goes into "fight or flight" mode to protect itself. The nerve "trees," or dendrites, get activated to sense harm. An electrical charge happens under pressure. Nitric oxide (NO) chemically reacts with oxygen (O_2) and creates a free radical known as *peroxynitrite* (ONOO). This chemical reaction is called, brace yourself, the "Devil's Triangle" (which appears as an upside-down triangle). If you know anything about free radicals, you know they damage our DNA (aka "seed" of the natural). Free radicals within our bloodstream, cause inflammation which can ultimately lead to disease processes and malformations of cells. There you have it, one of many examples of what the knowledge of evil/fear can do to our physical bodies. I think it's no coincidence that stress is the leading cause of heart disease, either. It's the corruption/curse of the flesh. We have to keep in mind the power that the spiritual realm has on the natural domain. We are so focused on the things that we see. We don't think the things that we don't see even exist. Many invisible things influence much of our day-to-day. Just because we haven't felt, been aware, or awakened to the unseen realm doesn't mean that it doesn't exist.

Do you know that scientists recently discovered and are unraveling the matter that holds together our very existence in the universe? They call it the "God particle" and to me, it's because of undeniable reasons. Secular scientists formally call it the Higgs Boson particle. The previous model of an atom used to be considered a solid form. Because our technology was limited to what we could zoom in on at a quantum level, we couldn't see what is now understood to be an infinite existence. Let me explain further what this means. Consider a circle. It's a finite confined space, meaning it has a limited closed in border. However, if you were to divide it by placing multiple circles within the circles, you could continue to do that infinitely as you zoomed in—endless circles within circles.

The same concept applies within an atom. Scientists have discovered that there is an infinite number of subatomic particles that make up more particles and so on. All these things are brought together and connected within a finite space by force. This force of matter is what we call "space" and is invisible to our naked eye. Our bodies are only solid to touch because of the infinite number of cells and particles within one another that are tightly drawn in by a magnetic force. Did you know that this so called "invisible space" makes up 99.99999% of all that exists? Yes, that's right only .0000001% of the makeup of our universe is what we physically see. We base our entire existence and beliefs, mostly on .0000001% of what exists! That means 99.99999% of the unseen realm controls what is physically seen. God is the driving force of existence. Side note go count those nines. Yep, you counted seven!

Not only does this exist at a quantum level within our bodies, but at an astrophysical level within outer space as well. Everything consists of dots within dots drawn in together by a magnetic force. The patterns of matter that exist within the infinitely vast expanse of space are the identical infinite pat-tern within our bodies, all drawn in together by this same "force." This force spins in a spiral-like mode and acts as a vacuum. Our galaxy and the patterns of the planets within, spin in the same spiral pattern as do our DNA. There are many mirrored images in space and nature, mimicking the patterns in the subatomic particles of our bodies. Everything is so specific and intricate. Shapes, patterns, numbers, as-trological signs within space, they are all so detailed. There is no way anyone can convince me that there is not a Cre-ator of it all. These things just don't happen. Not in the intri-cate, repeating patterns that it has. This "force" is within everything and holds together —everything.

Want to know something else cool? These same scientists identify the structure of this "God particle" force as a tetrahedron, which is a 3-D triangle shape. I think it's no coincidence that God is also represented as a triangle (Father, Son, Holy Spirit). To make it even cooler, when the triangle spins within the spiral force, it creates a reflection of itself and appears as the image of a star, just like the Star of David. Insert mind blown emoji here! Remember when I said God has multiple forms? His character is reflected within the very nanoparticles of existence. We have to get out of our limited concept of the bearded man sitting on the throne. God's existence is the force within everything.

So, there you have it, a mediocre explanation of God's infinite existence within our space and time. He is everywhere, working for our good.

• CHAPTER 3 •

Making Tent

One of the very next themes that I remember God drawing my attention to was the concept surrounding the "tabernacle." There are many references to it in the Bible, so I was on a mission from the get-go to find out the purpose of everything He considered significant. I was tired of having a shallow concept that would lead me to disregard and ignore the power behind His dwelling place. And, I kept hearing, "make tent with Me." I needed to find out what that meant. In one of the first dreams I had, God helped me discover the Tabernacle's profound symbolism and characteristics and His holy presence residing there. In my dream, I was in

Israel next to the Jordan River, standing on steps that led down into the river. The water was rushing and flooding everything around it. The weather was stormy and raining hard.

There was a local tour guide with me and others who surrounded me. He then walked straight up in the middle of the rushing river. I remember him calling me into the river, telling me to "come." It was like he wanted us to get baptized in the river. I was hesitant at first because the water was rough, and I didn't want to be swept away. I was almost frightened because it appeared overwhelming. When I looked at the people with me, I saw a woman next to me who seemed to be strong in her ways. She had a particular look about her and didn't seem like she would give in too easily. I turned to look behind me and saw a group of people partying. When I looked back at the tour guide, he knew that I was hesitant to step in. He then repeated three or four times, "Don't worry about the manna; worry about the hannah." I was like, "what the heck does that mean"? I didn't know, but I do remember feeling at peace to step in. I immediately turned to everyone around me and said, "come on, it will be okay." We stepped in, and then I woke up.

I instantly started looking at the significance of water and the Jordan River. Then it hit me, "Duh, that's where John baptized Jesus"! That's where the Holy Spirit presented Himself as a dove over Jesus. It was something that symbolized God's presence that would be made available to all when Jesus' body would be made glorified through the death at the cross. It was symbolic of the key given to us that directly would be used to open the portal to heaven straight into the throne room of God. Because of Jesus, we all have access to His Holy Spirit. The Jordan River symbolized the renewal of becoming a new creation through His Holy presence. It was symbolic of the promise to the people who choose Him to reap their time of harvest. It was a promise to reach His perfect kingdom. Jesus was thirty-three at the time. I was thirty-three when I had the dream. In fact, it was the very week I turned thirty-three, yet another cool way God showed Himself to me. God's Holy Spirit, in the form of a dove, manifested Himself upon Jesus the moment He was submerged in the water. God has shown me through Scripture that He represents Himself many times as water. That's why there's significance in getting baptized in water. It's a symbol of cleansing and "rebirth" of our spirit;

the old flesh man goes down under the water, and the new spiritual man comes up.

Before I go into the meaning of the whole "manna hannah" thing, I want to show you a little more of the significance of the water theme. I'll mention just a few Scriptures that compare His Holy Spirit to water. If you break apart the first few verses in Genesis 1, you will see that God created "firmament" in the waters. In the Hebrew, firmament means an expanse. This expanse separated the "waters from the waters." That tells me that the Spirit of God was flowing freely within the waters from the beginning. Genesis 2:6-7 states, "There went up a mist from the Earth, and watered the whole face of the ground. The Lord God formed man of the dust." John 7:37—39 says, "If anyone is thirsty, let him come to Me and drink. He who believes in Me, from his innermost being will flow rivers of living water. But this He spoke of the Spirit, whom those who believed in Him were to receive." There are hundreds of Scriptures where the water is symbolic of the Holy Spirit.

Before I looked up the last Scripture that I stated from John, I had another dream the next night. In this dream, I heard a voice say "John" and "Hebrews." That's when I opened the Bible and turned to both Books. Jesus is explaining the pathways to the Father through Him in the Spirit when He leaves the physical Earth to sit at the right hand of the Father. The Scriptures reiterated the theme of the renewal and purification of us by the Holy Spirit through baptism. We didn't have access to the Holy Spirit until the day of Pentecost when He was poured out on the disciples in the upper room. He sent His Spirit to us when He left the Earth. Now that Jesus is in the throne room of the Father, He made a pathway of access to that place when we choose Him as Savior and Lord. That access is His Spirit through prayer. And baptism is represented as a pathway for His presence to move in us through the water.

I think it's no coincidence that frequencies move easier in the molecular structure of water. Frequencies are vibrations that move, impact, and form matter. I think it's also cool that the structure of water is in the shape of a triangle as well. The frequencies His presence puts out moves through water and into our physical beings. He makes way for the spiritual to be reflected in the natural.

Let's go back to the "manna hannah" thing. What the heck was this silly little thing that I heard the tour guide say in my dream? I knew it had to mean something. Sure enough, it meant more than I could ever realize. "Manna" is the actual supply sent from heaven. Back in the desert, when the Israelites escaped out of Egypt to head into the land that God promised them, they wandered around for forty years. The reason is that they kept ignoring the commands of God. They proved themselves rebellious and stubborn by not fully trusting and submitting to the Father's voice. They weren't ready to enter the Promised Land. They were worried about starving to death and more concerned about what they lacked. They doubted God. So, they focused on the fleshly matters of surviving. Because God found favor in Moses through his daily pursuit of Him, He honored Moses' prayer to provide for the Israelites. Manna, heavenly food, was sent down from heaven to feed the children of Israel.

Manna also represents the supply that God gives us to meet our needs. Check this out from John 6:58, "This is that bread which came down from heaven: not as your fathers did eat manna and are dead; he that eateth of this bread shall live forever." Jesus is saying, stop worrying about what you are lacking. Stop worrying about the supply that you have or don't have, but focus on me, your spiritual food. Come to me first. In fact, that's what "Hannah" means. Hannah, in Hebrew, means "grace." More specifically, Hannah symbolized what it meant to "make tent within the Holy Spirit." Hannah was a woman devoted to the Lord and trusted in His promises for her. Even though she was barren and what the world might view as hopeless, she believed that God was in her life for good. She understood how to reverence the incredible power of God no matter what the circumstance. Hannah found favor with God so He fulfilled His promise to allow her to birth Samuel. She trusted God and spent her life in His presence not only before the promise was manifested, but after the promise as well. She didn't cease even after the promise was fulfilled. She dedicated her son to the tent tabernacle of God's presence. She knew how incredible God's presence is and giving her son to God wasn't just a gift to Him, it was a gift to her son too. Nothing is better than being in the presence of the Spirit of God. Hannah was the perfect example of someone who immerses their life in the tent of His presence. What does "making tent" mean? It means recognizing His presence that is housed within us. It means allowing that presence to bring us incredible power to utilize for the betterment of ourselves and others.

Much of the book of John and Hebrews' recurring themes place much focus around grace and becoming one with the Holy Spirit. Being a tent for the Holy Spirit means that we humble ourselves by taking away the focus of our needs and what we are lacking. We just spend time with Him, as discussed in chapter one. When we pursue Him, He shows us His character. When we learn about His personality, we become more like Him. We become one with Him. Something happens when we start studying the Word and go to Him to love and reverence Him. He fills us with a sense of completion. We begin to realize we have all we need in Him. It's hard to put into words because my words will never do His Spirit justice, but you'll know what I mean when you make time for Him.

That feeling you get on the inside, that still small voice you hear, that strong tug on your insides directing your every move, that's Him. You continue to confirm that it's Him by turning to Scripture when you hear and feel certain things.

You allow your body to become a living tabernacle/tent that houses Him. You become one with Him. He is the ultimate true sanctuary housed within us. When I turned to Hebrews, I saw that current theme again. Hebrews 8:2 says, "A minister, and of the true tabernacle, which the Lord pitched, and not man." Notice the word "pitched." We pitch tents, right? So why a tent? When the Israelites were in the desert, they pitched a tent tabernacle to house the presence of God. Because of man's fall in the garden, God had to create access to Him through a specific direction within the tent tabernacle. That's why He ultimately sent Jesus in human form to create a permanent pathway to His presence from Earth to heaven for us later. Hebrews 9:8, "The Holy Ghost this signifying, that the way into the holiest of all was not yet made manifest, while as the first tabernacle was yet standing." Jesus became the permanent access so we could live in the presence and power of God, which is now readily available to all who believe and choose to receive it. Once the body of Jesus was glorified, He made a portal of sorts for us to feel God's presence. He did this by sending the "Comforter," which is the Holy Spirit (John 15:26). 1 Corinthians 3:16 says we are His temple, "Don't you know that you yourselves are God's temple and that God's Spirit dwells in your midst"? He wants to give us access here on Earth to His throne room. We become the tent that houses the presence of God. The tent is moveable. The Israelites were able to take the presence of God with them everywhere they went. God uses the story of the tent within the desert as a representation for us to take Him wherever we go. We are the mobile tents that house the Holy Spirit.

I then started studying more into the original Tabernacle that was set up in the desert among them. The only people that were selected to manage the matters within the temple were the people who were actively making themselves clean through daily sacrifice. These were the Levites, the people who were fervently humbling themselves in total reverence towards the Father and His will. They were pure enough to come close to the presence of God to make sacrifices that redeemed the rest of the tribes of Israel. These people were explicitly handpicked and appointed by God. Not because He loved them more than others, but because they were diligently proving themselves devoted and clean enough to manage the sacredness of the Holy of Holies. They were daily repenting and sanctifying themselves before God. They understood His sacred power.

Remember, you can't mix the unclean with the clean. We make that separation through choice, not Him. He'll appoint us if we diligently seek Him and don't ignore His voice that guides us through His will. It's not that our desires don't matter. He's not trying to take that away. He knows the desires of our hearts. He has something even better for us within His will. As mentioned previously, we just can't see it fully looking through the spiritual limitations of our eyes.

Because of the righteous hearts of the Levites (meaning they pursue Him in every moment), God honored their prayers and sacrifices to redeem others. The Levites were the example for the others to follow. God used them to help turn the hearts of the rest of the Israelites, which is what the church is called to do. The church is to be the tour guide to introduce people to Jesus. We show them by demonstrating our reverence to Him, as we become one with Him. We live out His characteristics (fruits of the Spirit) to others. We allow the outpouring of His life-giving waters to open their eyes to the truth. We show them the love of the Father by becoming His love to others.

I heard "misinterpreting Scripture" right after hearing the word "John" in that dream. Well, John references the theme of grace a lot. When we hear the word "grace," we think of almost a justification of our sins. We think, "He loves and forgives us when we sin" because He can "take our sin away." All that is true, but it goes much deeper than that. If you don't look closely into what that truly means, you'll take His grace for granted. You will find yourself still focusing on the desires of your flesh over and over, just expecting Him to forgive you after. You don't maliciously try to make that happen; it just does when you don't really understand the deeper meaning of what grace is.

He has shown me a deeper meaning to the concept of grace. It's something that represents the supernatural power of His Holy Spirit. When you search Scriptures that reference His grace it reflects what I am sharing. Like I said, He has many forms and more profound symbolism. Yes, forgiveness and mercy fall under the umbrella of grace, but that's just part of it. Grace is something that is so much more powerful than what we realize. Ephesians 4:7 says, "But to each one of us grace has been given as Christ apportioned it." Hebrews 4:16, "...so that we may receive mercy and find grace to help us in our time of need." Acts 18:27, "...which had believed through grace." 2 Corinthians

12:9, "My grace is sufficient for you, for my power is made perfect in weakness." All these Scriptures reference a deeper concept of grace. It's profound; it's the power of His Spirit. His grace acts as a supernatural power within us to see others as HE sees them. It's so we can see OURSELVES as He sees us. His grace also empowers us to OVERCOME our sin. Not to continue in it but to be delivered from it.

He's calling us to draw near to Him, because in "making tent" with God, we have access to His supernatural power through the Holy Spirit to overcome ALL. Hebrews 10:22, "Let us draw near with a true heart in full assurance of faith, having our hearts sprinkled from an evil conscience, and our bodies washed with pure water." His Spirit is "pure water." Paul writes that we are the body of Christ, and Jesus is the head. If we are His body, then we possess His power to overcome. He takes away the shame of sin. He even takes away the thoughts that corrupt our state of mind that prevent fulfillment. That's genuinely becoming Christ-like, which is what He GIVES us when we seek HIM FIRST, not through any other channels. We don't become Christ-like through our ways, but His. We can't keep letting the lies that surround us keep us from the truth. The truth that we have all that we need through Him.

Revelation 22:17, "And the Spirit and the bride say, Come. And let him that heareth say, Come, And, let him that is athirst come. And whosoever will let him take the water of life freely." The tour guide in my dream was directing me and those around me into the waters of life. Everyone has access to Him; all we have to do is "COME" and step in. Let's be the tour guide for people to draw them near to His presence. He's calling us to trust His waters, step in, and cross the Jordan to enter into what He's promised us.

• CHAPTER 4 •

Rise Up Levites

Before I start this chapter, I want to give you some background on why I believe God spoke to me about the Levites. As you will read, they were a set apart group of people who were wholly given to the service of God's sanctuary, His presence, and His glory. They were the priests of the Old Testament and still today are the priests of God's Temple in Jerusalem. For the church, believers of today, we are called to be like the Levites; set apart for His service. Interesting enough, the word "church" in the original language was "ekklesia" meaning the called-out ones. We are to be separated to God just like the Levites are too. In addition, Peter wrote, "...you are a chosen generation, a royal priesthood, a holy nation, His own special people, that you may proclaim the praises of Him who called you out of darkness into His marvelous light" (1 Peter 3:9).

I kept hearing over and over repeatedly in my head, "Rise up the Levites," "Rise up the Levites." Through His repetitive urging, I knew God was telling me to play a part in the awakening of His appointed ones. The Levites, as I mentioned in chapter three, were the priests of God, who pitched the Tabernacle tent, and they played a significant role when it came to gathering people to praise God. Before I get into their specific functions, I want to point out something that God showed me in the book of Revelation.
In Revelation, Chapter 3, John is speaking with the angel of the Lord. The Spirit of Christ, in the form of an angel, instructed him to write letters to the angels that watched over specific churches. These churches, I believe, represent seven significant symbols for us to learn from today. The churches, in one of the many layers of this reference, represent the phases and groups that believers fall into. They became distinguished amongst one another

through their behaviors and traits in which they presented themselves to God. When you read the letters in Revelation, you can grasp why. The behaviors of each church seemed to morph into characteristics based on the influence of the culture around them. Ultimately, their behaviors were influenced by which spirit they were being manipulated by. At least that's what I interpret when I read the letters. It's very similar to what we experience today. I believe God uses these churches in Revelation as an application for us to reference from. He uses the letters to show us the characteristics that are useful for His kingdom, the characteristics that will win souls, and bring life and fulfillment to us. God doesn't settle for mediocre when it comes to the outcome of His promises to His children. To me, He uses these letters as an outline to become the best version of ourselves in Him. Sometimes betterment requires a little tough love spoken in truth. I don't know about you, but I can handle a little constructive criticism if it's going to lead me to the most fulfilling eternal life possible. Though some of the letters are tough to read, they somehow provide me with a hope. They're reflective of a wake-up call for a second chance. It's God telling us that He's reaching out even in our mistakes.

One church, in particular, stood out to me, the Church of Laodicea. I think many modern-day churchgoers have found ourselves in this group. The angel describes this church as "lukewarm, worried about riches, blind and naked, in need of nothing." Behaviors that reveal these believers won't take a stand for what's right in God's eyes. They coast along and live according to what the world can provide them. They are driven by the natural. They have forgotten about the 99.99999% of the unseen that affects their existence. They're worried about what they have or what they can achieve. They may not be super passionate either way. They feel good by surrounding themselves with good things, but they don't dive deeper. They are superficial and lukewarm in their beliefs. They want to mind their own business and coast along peacefully.

I believe many of us have come to feel this way in church. It's not surprising that this was the last letter written to the churches. And, by the tone of the message, Jesus is not fond of this mentality. What will lukewarm get you? Lukewarm believers barely survive. It makes room for the enemy to win over our souls. We weren't created to be destroyed. He created us to be overcomers and to have an abounding life of extravagant love in Him. Just like I don't want to raise my kids to feel weak and insignificant, God doesn't raise His kids to be that either. We are meant for so much more than half-hearted living. He's not attacking this group to shun them; He's correcting this group of believers to awaken them so they can repent and turn back to the purpose He has for them. We often look at the negative side of things. We get defensive. It's because we haven't gotten to know the character of God, so we misinterpret Him in our thinking. Remember, He works for our good (Romans 8:28).

Anytime I need help understanding how He sees me; I think of my kids. I adore my kids. I only want what's best for them. No matter what they may do, I will ALWAYS love them and will embrace them when they come to me. Sometimes my love requires me to correct their behavior so that I can direct them to a better path. They may not like it at first, but when they get to see what I have been trying to show them, finally, they appreciate it so much more. As a result, I see an increased passion and excitement in them. That's exactly how God handles us. Just like Psalms 103:13 says, "Like as a father pitieth his children, so the Lord pitieth them that fear Him." The prodigal son story is also a prime example of God's goodness towards His creation.

I honestly believe that He is calling on the "Levites," the remnant of believers who are drawing near to Him, to gather His children. He wants to gather ALL His children together so He can fulfill His plan and make His glory known to the world. He's ready to take back what the enemy has stolen from us and ultimately Him. The only way for Him to make Himself fully known is when His "Levites" are ready to fully display His glory (His power and presence).

The Levites represent the "oil & wine," according to Nehemiah 13:5, which was prescribed for the Levites, who were singers and gatekeepers. That's why I think Revelation 9:4 commands the winds not to harm anything during the Tribulation until He seals those who are called to be intercessors for those who are lost. The awakening to call forth life and love upon the lives of others starts with the remnant. Those who remain faithful and fervent for God in every season. They minister hope and victory to those around them which comes through Jesus. They show others how to fervently seek the Father so they can understand the "mysteries" of His will.

I believe that there are appointed times in all His doings. Scripture states that in "these days" (last days), He will reveal the mysteries of the heavens to those who have an "ear" to hear and understand (Luke 8:10). It's for those who are diligently seeking and carefully listening to His Spirit. His character is only looking to bring life, not destruction. He's calling for a daily sanctification of our souls, which is a daily repentant and humbled heart. Just as the Levites were diligent about acknowledging that God's presence deserved their best, we are called to give to God the same thing right now. This time is so imminent for us to utilize everything He has purposed for us. The more we are humbled and willing to listen, the more He's going to give us.

Our pride is the dam that blocks His rushing waters of life and abundance. He gives us an outpouring when we break that dam. We need His living water. The world needs an outpouring of hope that overflows from those who choose to allow Him to consume them. The enemy is in full force right now, and the church needs to rise-up so believers can show others life and protection in Christ. He's longing to set up His kingdom to remove the suffering and evil from the world. For each soul sanctified in Him, it's one more piece of heaven that is reflected here on Earth. We demonstrate heaven on Earth through our daily living, and He's given us the keys to open the doors of heaven (Matthew 16:19).

That was the duty of the Levites in the Old Testament. They were appointed to gather the tribes together for the sanctification of their sins through repentance. They were drawing others near to undo what their sins and wickedness had brought to the land. The wicked were making sacrifices to other gods and trying to create alternate pathways to become gods themselves. They were corrupting the holy lands and temples of God (2 Chronicles 29:16). They were allowing Satan to bring destruction upon them. Everything people chose to do that was displeasing to God, He used His priests to undo through animal sacrifice. It had to be undone so they could have access to Him. He was reversing the perversion of the enemy. God was teaching them how to claim back what the enemy was stealing from them, which was the good that He was trying to bring to the people of Israel. He wasn't commanding the Israelites to perform all these crazy sacrifices for no reason. There is a reason for it all, even if we don't understand it.

God created a pathway to Him, through Jesus' perfect sacrifice on the Cross, which made the unclean, clean again through faith in Jesus. It was all for our good. Joshua 3:5, "Sanctify yourselves: for tomorrow, the Lord will do wonders among you." Why did God send His Son for the final sacrifice? He made a way for the harvest. Later, I'll have an entire chapter dedicated to the day of harvest because it's a complete fulfillment of His glory, when He calls the nations to be transformed so He can establish a new heavens and Earth. It deserves a whole section of its own. I'll give you a little taste though, Psalms 102:16, "When the Lord shall build up Zion, He shall appear in His glory."

All we have to do is WAKE UP. We must RISE UP. If we make His glory and His LIFE-GIVING grace known to others around us, their eyes and ears will be opened. Psalms 138:4, "All the kings of the Earth shall praise thee, O Lord, when they hear the words of thy mouth." The "kings of the Earth" that are referenced in the Old Testament were wicked. They tried to achieve a godlike status through their strength and control over people. How much more powerful is that Scripture now? Even the blinded eyes and the deaf ears will hear His voice and praise! We can't limit God's power and grace. He is going to turn the armies that come against us. All will see His power.

The "Levites" are called to direct the lost to Him. It is God's will for NOT ONE of His sheep to be lost (Matt. 18:14). John 6:39, "And this is the will of Him who sent me, that I shall lose none of all those He has given me but raise them up at the last day." The righteous (those who are one with Him) are called to gather people in the last days harvest. When you're following His will and demonstrating His TRUE and LOVING heart, people WILL listen. Proverbs 11:5—11 says that the paths of the wicked will lead to their own destruction. They bring on the destruction themselves. They don't realize the goodness God has for them, so they fight against Him. It is up to the righteous to cover them with prayer and become active vessels outpouring the love of Jesus over them. Verse 11 says, "By the blessing of the upright the city is exalted: but it is overthrown by the mouth of the wicked." To me, this means that we hold the power to overcome the path of the wicked in order to save the nations for Him. We can flip the perspective that leads to the path of destruction over ourselves and others if we choose to utilize the power, He has given us. 2 Chronicles 20:6 is also reflective of this. "And said, O Lord God of our fathers, art not thou God in heaven? And rules not thou over all the kingdoms of the heathen? And in thine hand is there not power and might, so that none is able to withstand thee?" Some Christians only focus on the destruction and division part in many of these similar passages. They should be working with the plan of God for salvation through faith in Jesus. God told me it's all in how we look at it. If you are looking at it through His life-giving character and will, you will see that He longs to save, even the ones who are blinded by the enemies' ways. He has appointed believers to go to bat for the salvation of the wicked. I'll expand on that later. We can shift the pathway of destruction. When we focus on the destruction of others, like the minds of the blind will do, it WILL cause destruction, even within our households.

However, when we see others through the lens of grace, His glory will exalt ALL. Romans 3:23, "We have ALL fallen short of the glory of God." Then Joel 1:14, "Sanctify ye a fast, call a solemn assembly, gather the elders and all the inhabitants of the land into the house of the Lord your God, and cry unto the Lord." The "Levites" always planned a fast and/or feast to prepare to go before the Lord. They did this for the sanctification of the tribes of Israel. The moment we submit our selfish ways to see His better ways, we will see people differently and desire God's plan for them. Luke 2:21, "When the days of her purification according to the law of Moses were accomplished, they brought him to Jerusalem, to present him to the Lord."

The "Levites" were called the gatekeepers of God's kingdom. Deuteronomy 14:27, Ezra 2:70, and Nehemiah 7:13, among so many other Scriptures, state that the "Levites" were managers of the gate. What does that mean? Well, the Kingdom of Heaven is separated by a wall of the natural. It's separated by the wall that the world has created from God. However, God makes a way to go through these gates to get to Him. He made that way through Jesus. Jesus became the gatekeeper who opens the gate to eternal life with His Father. When we become one with Jesus, in essence, He uses us to be managers of the gates as well. We show others a way in to be with the Father. Through a "sacrifice of praise" and humbled heart of thanksgiving we enter His presence and glory. Psalm 100:4, "Enter into His gates with thanksgiving, and into his courts with praise." That is the blueprint of how we should approach His Throne room: humbled and praising Him. We, who represent the "Levites", cry out in praise to turn the ways of the wicked to the Lord. Scripture says they are given power over ALL flesh. In that appointed day, why would God hold back?

To someone who may be reading this and is still confused by what this all means and how something we can't see might be manifested, I URGE you to go to Him and ask Him for more clarity. Just last year, I didn't fully understand what all of this meant. However, I had faith that He existed and trusted that He is working for my good even when I may not see or feel it. I just kept pursuing Him. Now, I am writing a book on the journey He took me on. I'm so excited about the pathway He has prepared for you if you allow Him to show you. It's time for believers to gather together as one in Spirit to demonstrate an outpouring of His love. Rise up, Levites! Rise up!

• CHAPTER 5 •

Judgment

I don't know about you, but the word "judgment" use to make me cringe. It is because of the perspective we have developed around it. Every day we battle with operating through the mindset of what the world has created this word to be. Want to know something? God intended it for good. Now, this thought may confuse you a bit. It makes me think of the "judgments" God unleashed upon the land of Egypt and the "destruction" that the book of Revelation discusses. Yes, it was and will be very ugly; ugly within the pathway of Satan and those who choose him. Here's the thing though, it's really Satan who brought this judgment upon those who follow him. They made the choice because of their free will.

He gave them the cursed lens to look through. The outpouring of judgment is against all evil and those who participate in it. However, there is a purpose in it. God wants to purify people so they can see life. Remember, God has to get rid of evil in order for us to live without suffering. Satan wants people to believe that God is bad and judgmental. And quite frankly, he wants people to think there is no God. Satan wants people to worship him. God is begging people to reach for life in Him. It's not because He is selfish like Satan, it's the opposite. He wants everyone to live filled with an all-consuming joy. When you choose to walk outside the lens of life with God, you feel an emptiness, even if you can't fully explain it. There's always a desire to reach for more because you will never feel satisfied. Fulfillment is never achieved within Satan's plan.

Judgment actually has the potential to purify and produce everlasting life. When you ignore the voice of God, the pathway is destruction. It's because the lies of the cursed flesh will blind us to the consequence, which is death. Satan tries to drag us to death with him. What we fail to do is look deeper into those Scriptures that refer to "destruction." When we lean on the Father, He shows us that beyond the destruction and the wrath is mercy for those who will repent and believe in Jesus. Trusting in Him takes away the strongholds of Satan, who is trying to appoint us to destruction with him. In all, INCLUDING what appears to be destruction, there is a purpose. It's all for His glory to be seen, which is for us to love and be loved. God doesn't bring destruction; He allows it. He puts it in our hands. He gave us free will, remember? When people disobey God, they open a door for Satan to attack and destroy them. He blinds and deceives people all the time because they are ignoring God. People create a wall between themselves and God, thereby removing themselves from His comfort and protection, creating a separation. Remember, it is impossible for God to mix with the unclean because that would make Him corrupted. Again, it's not that He doesn't love them or doesn't want to be with them. That's why He makes a continuous way for everyone to find Him through Jesus.

Jesus became sin, overcame it, and created a pathway to God through His sacrifice. I believe that even within the "destruction" of the wicked ways, He can and will make people new who turn from the skewed perception that Satan has given them. Even in the destruction He can make a way for people to receive Christ and obtain an abundant, incredible, everlasting life with Him. He provides a way when there seems no way. All we have to do is choose Him. Jesus defeated death, and with God, it holds no power. The concept of death goes way beyond what we see in the natural. God doesn't see death for those who choose Him. That's why Scriptures reference those who have passed being "asleep." He sees a transition from this life into a greater life. The freedom in knowing that the grave no longer holds us down is so powerful.

Sometimes believers will segment out Scriptures and focus on the judgment part. It's so sad, especially when it happens within the four walls of the church. We read "judgment," "judgment," "judgment," and we think it's our responsibility to judge. Often people leave the church because they feel shame from the judgment of man rather than being guarded in truth and love. Now hear me, I am not making a sweeping generalization here. Some churches and believers walk in the love of God, especially those who have been through hard places where they have overcome. Those who have received much grace tend more to extend grace to others. But, unfortunately, there are still believers who don't have the revelation that "mercy triumphs over judgment" (James 2:13).

People hurt by judgment often run away, feeling the weight of their sin and the potential punishment from it. They run to things of the world because the devil creates a mirage of finding acceptance, giving life, and temporary fulfillment. Ezekiel 13:22 says, "Because with lies ye have made the heart of the righteous sad, whom I have not made sad; and strengthened the hands of the wicked that he should not return from his wicked way, by promising him life." We are all considered wicked when we choose the devil's temptations. And, of course, we will want to run toward what appears to be life-giving when we feel shame. However, that's what the devil wants you to believe. It's so crucial for us to rest our hope on Christ and not man, even men within the church. It's also just as vital for us to be able to gather together as one in Christ because His glory will exude ever more powerful. That's the real heart of the church, to be able to gather in His presence to honor His glory.

Here is how judgment gets twisted. God revealed to me that we misunderstand the purpose of judgment and what He is hopeful it will produce. Judgment isn't about bringing death to someone; it's about a hopeful expectation of bringing life to them. Before I get into that, let's look at three types of judgment. First, the world view judgment is unacceptable and destructive. Unbelievers will revolt against whatever they perceive as judgment. Then there is the religious kind of judgment like what we see the Pharisees of the Bible extending to people and situations. Lastly, there's what the Bible calls righteous judgment. There is a MAJOR difference between religious and righteous judgment. Righteous judgment operates out of Holy Spirit guidance. You are looking at others through God's lens of love and grace. You are always looking at them to save them, not to separate them from eternal life. We have to bring people with us to meet Jesus.

Do people always live their lives according to the Holy Spirit? Heck no! I know I don't. However, the moment we consider them unworthy to enter into the kingdom of heaven is the moment we put a block on ourselves to enter in as well. Matthew 7:2 says, "For with what judgment ye judge, ye shall be judged." I love looking at one particular interaction between David and King Saul in 1 Samuel 24. King

Saul previously tried to kill David because Satan deceived the King. Then the day came where the Lord delivered Saul into the hands of David. David had an opportunity to kill King Saul. It was a test to see what David would do. What did David do, however? He handed the judgment of Saul's destiny straight back to God (24:15). David declared that even though the Lord gave Saul to avenge David, David chose to spare his life. He pleaded to God, basically saying, "if you place judgment on him, place it on me as well." David understood that he was a sinner too. He was looking through the eyes of the Holy Spirit and realized his battle was not with flesh and blood, but with the evil spirits at work in the natural. 1 Samuel 18:10 says that "an evil spirit came upon Saul," which, as I mentioned, happens when you ignore God's direction. You make yourself vulnerable to affliction. David didn't blame King Saul. He blamed the spirit that was using him. By believing that judgment should come on him too, David basically laid down his life for the redemption of Saul. Isn't that a picture of what Jesus did for you and me? And like John 15:13 says, "No greater love hath no man than this, that a man lay down his life for his friends."

David did the same thing when it came to the judgment released upon people within his kingdom. He told God, "punish me, I'm their leader, punish me." David was willing to take on the punishment for all. Because of his humility and selflessness, God honored David's cry. He made a covenant, a promise to spare both David and Saul's seed and the seed of the kingdom. I think that's precisely why the Bible refers to Jesus as the "seed of David" and the "rod of Jesse" (David's father). David's righteousness was a direct reflection of God. Though David messed up multiple times, he continued to pick right back up to pursue the Father. He humbled himself. He was willing to take on the weight of the sin of his people. That's what God did by sending Jesus, "the seed of David." He sent Himself in human form to take on the weight of the sin of the world, His creation. It was His way of saying what David said, "I'm their king and redeemer; I will bear their punishment." It's why Jesus said right before He died, "Father forgive them for they know not what they do." The Spirit of God led David. And by God's actions in every case, we see that God's desire and character is always to save.

I genuinely believe that we can turn away the wrath of God in every situation by interceding and praising our Lord in victory to turn the hearts of those blinded by the evil. He has given us authority and dominion over the flesh. We are called to repay evil with good. That's how we can turn the mindset of those who come against us. They too long to be loved. When we operate out of righteous judgment, we can change hearts. That's what David did to Saul. Saul said in 1 Samuel 24:17, "Thou art more righteous than I: for thou has rewarded me good, whereas I have rewarded thee evil." Luke 6:32 says, "for sinners also love those that love them." Even Moses turned away the wrath of God's judgments on Israel. His prayer turned God's anger into mercy. Psalms 106:23, "Therefore He said that He would destroy them, had not Moses His chosen stood before Him in the breach, to turn away His wrath, lest He should destroy them." It takes a lot for God to cause wrath against a nation. That's why Scripture states He is "slow to anger." He's always looking for a way to save. That's His mission.

In Revelation, Scripture gives us a visual on fear of the Lord. Fear to understand how mighty He is and that yes, He does possess the power to destroy if He chooses. When we choose destruction, we get destruction. However, the fear of Him (humbling of ourselves before Him) finds favor from Him. When we submit, we bring forth our sin because we recognize it. The moment we acknowledge and repent, Jesus, our Intercessor, comes to take our sin away. Acts 8:33 says, "In his humiliation, his judgment was taken away." Psalms 19:9 also states, "The fear of the Lord is clean, enduring for ever: the judgments of the Lord are true and righteous altogether."

Have you ever thought that maybe, just MAYBE, the judgments are there to "cause the water to boil" in hopes to bring the fear of the Lord? The judgments are a call for life, not death. It's calling for the death of our old flesh, the knowledge of sin, and the spirits of darkness that follow it. In Revelation, it also refers to them getting consumed by the fire and that they will melt like wax. In other references, getting consumed by the fire of the Lord is a good thing. It's a refiner's fire. It purifies. Psalms 102:26, "They shall perish, but thou shalt endure: yea, all of them shall wax old like a garment: as a vesture shalt thou change them, and they shall be changed." When you look at this Scripture with a lens of judgment that brings death, all you see is the reference to death. Again, I remember what God told me, "It's all in how you see it." When I look at it with the lens of righteous judgment, I see the death of both the old flesh and the curse, not their soul. Hence, "wax old like a GARMENT." Why would it also say "they shall be changed" after it says "they shall perish"? We have to change our perspective of God. He is LIFE-GIVING to those who choose life. When we trust Him even while facing death, He brings life. Isaiah 33:22, "For the Lord is our judge; the Lord is our lawgiver, the Lord is our king; He will save us."

I vow to always look at His ways through His lens. Isaiah 59 is a perfect reflection. "Behold, the Lord's hand is not shortened, that it cannot save; neither His ear heavy, that it cannot hear." Right after this verse, He also states that it is us who cause the divide because we have made ourselves unclean. Because of that, we aren't ready to enter yet. Verse 59:9, "Therefore is judgment far from us, neither doth justice overtake us: we wait for light, but behold obscurity." Later in verses 15 and 16 he says, "the Lord saw it, and it displeased Him that there was no judgment. He saw that there was no man, and wondered that there was no intercessor." What did this mean? It means that Jesus hadn't come yet at this time to act as the intercessor for the redemption. He hadn't raised up His next generation "Levites" (You know us, the remnant, the intercessors on Earth.) to offer prayers and praise. Judgment in the eyes of the Lord, when received rightly by man, produces a GOOD thing. Isaiah 61:8, "For I, the Lord love judgment." It means that in His judgment, the old will be destroyed and made new. Everyone will see God's glory when wicked hearts turn to Christ. Which is why Jesus came, right? He said, "for I am not come to call the righteous, but the sinners to repentance."

I am certainly not saying we need to accept sin. I am not saying it's okay for us to live in sin. If we view Him so merciful and beautiful even to repay good to those who have forsaken Him, why the heck would we choose to dishonor Him daily through sin? We repent of our sin and submit to His will daily. Why? Because He protects us. He gives us peace through the trials of the world. When we walk with His Holy Spirit, He writes the law upon our hearts to know the difference between good and evil. The Spirit keeps us from harm. Scriptures say that He didn't come to destroy the law but to fulfill it. In Matthew 5:18, says that the law won't be fulfilled until the new heaven and Earth. At a time when sin will be destroyed for good. Until then, we need to know how to keep ourselves and those around us from getting hurt by sin. We overcome sin and Satan by the Blood of Jesus. His Blood keeps a hedge of protection over and around us. His Spirit becomes the "conscience" of our hearts. We don't accuse others with the knowledge of it, but we follow His Spirit to keep ourselves out of harm's way. The moment we make accusations and shame others because of their sin, we cooperate with and follow the spirit of the devil, who is called the "accuser of the brethren." It stems from what Adam and Eve did in the Garden. They never confessed and repented of their sin, they accused and blamed one another by saying, "she did it," "he did it." That's also why Jesus told the Pharisees when they were calling out the sins of others "ye are of your father the devil." We have a great responsibility when it comes to the law. Not to use it to accuse and point out the sin of others, but to keep ourselves and others from destruction. Heck, we don't live under the curse of the law, right? We've been delivered from the curse of sin and death. Jesus said, "IF you love me, you will keep My commandments." Under the law, we obeyed because we HAD TO. Under grace, we obey because we want to and because we love.

So, what do we do when we recognize that others aren't following God? We love them. Love doesn't accept sin; it COVERS sin. We show them Jesus. We share Christ with them and lead them to Him. We speak the truth in love. We allow the Holy Spirit filter to do the talking or even just the listening. On our own, without the help of the Holy Spirit, we can't help sinners because we are sinners ourselves. We have to turn to Him to give us guidance. Someone led us to Christ and life with Him, now we are the ones pointing others to Christ as well.

Always remember, "We ALL fall short of the glory of God." When we don't know what to do, we go to the Father. Luke 12:12 says, "For the Holy Ghost shall teach you in the same hour what ye ought to say." Trust Him; He will direct you when you listen to His voice. His voice may be a tug on the inside; it may be a dream; it may be through the words of another following Him. However He manifests Himself to you, just know He is there. Psalms 89:14 says, "Justice and judgment are the habitations of thy throne: mercy and truth shall go before thy face." In this verse, I believe He is saying mercy equals justice and judgment equals truth. The truth that He will fulfill all His promises. Well, if Scripture says

Jesus is the Truth, then judgment is a good thing for those who respond rightly. He has called the sinners to repent. Psalms 94:10, "Judgment shall return unto righteousness." He came to turn the hearts. He is righteous, and His judgments are just full of mercy and love.

• CHAPTER 6 •

Love

Mark 12:30 and 31, "Thou shalt love the Lord thy God with all thy heart and with all thy soul, and with all thy mind, and with all thy strength: this is the first commandment. The second is this, Thou shalt love thy neighbor as thyself. There is none other commandment greater than these."

I think it's pretty essential for us to grasp the concept within the two greatest commandments that the voice of God gives to us. These are instructions to live by every day of our life, but I also believe God's love is the key that opens the kingdom of heaven here on Earth. I think most of us have come to understand that giving love and being loved is the main ingredient of feeling fulfilled. However, I believe we are called to look beyond the day-to-day. We have to learn to be kingdom minded. How else are we going to bring heaven to Earth unless we start seeing and believing it? How do we bring heaven to Earth?

I love to envision my thoughts around the harvest's fulfillment—the day when God reigns in full glory to turn the hearts toward His throne. I picture what heaven is like in person. By faith, I believe God is real so much that I create a detailed picture of what He is like in my mind. When I do that, He makes Himself known. He gives me comfort and peace. He allows me to feel His protection, His joy, and His love. Suddenly, I see things so much more clearly. When I let go of the thoughts and inhibitions of the natural world around me, He reveals Himself to me. It's the greatest love I have ever known, and it grows more and more to an incomprehensible level with each day. It's something I never knew I could ever feel, or that it even existed. When I humble myself to feel His love, He shows me what life is supposed to be like here on Earth. The more intentional I practice that mindset every day, the more I learn to walk with Him every day. I start to see people and the world around me through the eyes of Jesus. That is something I have prayed for my whole life, "Lord let me see people through Your eyes." That's how I've learned that all He wants to do is give life, not take it away. He wants us to walk next to Him, not be cast away from Him. Think of the Garden again. When you read the beginning of Genesis, what do you focus on the most? Did you give more focus to the casting out part? Did you ask, "why the heck did they eat the fruit, and why would God allow it"? Did you find yourself focusing on the negative? That's exactly what Satan wants you to look at, which is precisely what he did with me.

God's purpose is love, life, and belonging. Satan's purpose is pain, death, and division. He comes to kill, steal, and destroy. He is the father of lies. How do I know that God doesn't bring death? It's because the closer I got to Him, I felt life and peace, even in my darkest moments, when the world around me made me want to give up. That was the example that Job left us. It was to prove that through utter turmoil, God can still make you feel joy. Now we can see life from a different perspective. You no longer view the trial as a thing to get in your way and make you fall; you see it as something that makes you stronger. The moment you trust that He is still working behind the scenes for your good, He will give you a glimpse of what it looks like past the trial out ahead of you. And, He will display it right in front of your face. When you see that glimpse of joy and hope outside of the trial, you can press on with confidence and peace. You even view death differently. When you become kingdom-minded, you don't see death as the end, you see it as the beginning. You learn the true meaning of walking in victory and becoming an overcomer.

God uses what the devil brought to you and turns it for your good. We live in a cursed world brought on by choosing not to listen to God, which brings life. God is the one Who gives life, not us, and certainly not Satan, which is what the Scripture, "Whoever tries to keep their life will lose it, and whoever loses their life will preserve it" means. When WE, on our own, try to seek out or preserve our life without being one with Christ, our path will lead us to harm. It's because, in the natural, we don't see what could hurt us in the unseen. I think in this current culture, we can all agree that there are deep unexplainable things that we can't deny, the things that we cannot see. When we set our minds on Him,

He opens our eyes to see those things that come to destroy us.

You may ask, "why do God loving people get hurt then"? "If He loves us, why does He allow hurt"? It happens because the devil knows we are getting stronger in Christ to come against him. He's going to do everything He can to take you out. I know this seems scary. I've been there and honestly, it's a daily thing I face. God knows that our first reaction is to be afraid. That's why He continues to build our faith and strength as we keep pursuing Him. We can't give up in the face of fear. We have to face it. You see, the only power that Satan has on us is fear. When we give focus to it, his power grows. The moment we realize "greater is He who is in me than he who is in the world" (1 John 4:4), the big nasty beast he first appeared to be gets smaller. We realize that our fear creates an illusion that makes him look much bigger than he is. God gave us a free will to choose His relentless love and protection. Our power against Satan is only as big as our power to choose to rely on God for strength. I'll expand on that when I discuss our roles in spiritual warfare and authority later.

Another thing that is hard for people to understand is the whole servant and master concept. Again, the lies of Satan tell us that servanthood is about bondage to someone. We don't like bondage. Well, it's because we were not created for it. The Devil is just trying to steal from creation, twisting the truth. Servanthood is not demeaning. Man's perceptions brought that concept to fruition. Jesus said in Matthew 20:28, "Even as the Son of man did not come to be served, but to serve, and to give His life as a ransom for many." God's intention to serve someone wasn't to be considered less worthy of them. It was to develop humility and show love to them. To serve or love someone, even when they don't deserve it, is the ultimate form of sacrifice that produces strength. When your value is found in God, you don't rely on how others treat you for your happiness. You begin to allow yourself to show love to others expecting nothing in return from them because the love you have through Jesus is all you need. Servanthood to God and others isn't about feeling and being beneath them. It's about feeling and being love. To love is to lead. To lead in love is to become a true master. So, you must master servanthood with love. You become a master in the art of the greatest power on Earth AND in heaven, the art of love.

People who hurt are in hurting themselves. They just want to feel loved. Think about when you're in a relationship with someone. When I fight with my husband, I tend to lash out in anger because, in my perspective, he hurt me. I feel hurt because I care. Deep down, I just want to be loved and feel valued by him. The thing is, humans hurt and disappoint others all the time. It's because they are subjected to the Devil's lies all the time. That's why it is so important to rely on how God values us. He only brings worth to us. So many marriages and friendships fail because we believe lies. Sometimes the lies come from the voice inside of our head. Sometimes it comes as the voice of others. However, only one liar is masking behind it all, and that's Satan.

Relationships with others can quickly become a game of who can hold out in pride the longest. We place our happiness and security on the head of the other person. A responsibility that is not theirs to manage, only God's. The moment I started to apply that within my marriage, it immediately took a 180 turn. God began to redeem my marriage. It was because I was seeing my husband as a child of God. A person who just wants to be loved like me. Think about it. When we are angry, what is the one thing that will break it?

LOVE! It doesn't matter how much my husband ticks me off. The moment he surrenders to love me regardless of what his emotions might be making him feel, my wall of defense crumbles. All it may take is a hug or even a touch of his hand. You feel when the person's heart surrenders. Nothing changed when I placed the responsibility on him to make the first move. It's because he was probably expecting the same from me. That's what happens when we are hurt, we don't want to surrender. We want the other person to make the first move. When I treat him how I would want to be treated, that's when change and transformation happened. People don't call it the "golden rule" for nothing. Proverbs 10:12, "Hatred stirs up strife, but love covers all offenses."

I think a big thing we miss many times is being able to recognize our pride and call it what it is. Our pride is the resistance we feel on the inside, not to forgive. It's the resistance we feel that delays us in showing love to someone, even when they don't deserve it. We can't choose to love based on if the other person deserves it or not. When we do that, we transform love into pride. Showing love doesn't always mean admitting you're wrong. It's merely showing love. We have to bring it back to simplicity. We overcomplicate the situation when we submerge ourselves in our emotions and thoughts. The Devil thrives within those hidden places inside of us. The moment I choose to be the first to give in and embrace my husband with love, both of our walls collapse. It's not about who's right or wrong. The only thing wrong is letting pride get in the way of love.

Why do we view surrender as a weakness? It's probably because when we have the mindset of putting our happiness first, we will always see it that way. That's what happens when our security is placed on anything other than God. Our perspective is selfish in nature. We can deny it all we want. The moment we place our worth in Christ is the moment our lives will BRING life.

Submitting our pride to put others first is not saying that our happiness doesn't matter. We have to stop viewing it that way. Happiness and fulfillment come from submitting and putting aside our pride, which causes division. What was the very thing that separated Lucifer from God? It was his pride. His "pride came before his fall." Our pride is the very thing that limits us. Let me clarify a little bit about what I mean when I say "pride" because so often our perspective can get skewed. We confuse FEELING "proud" with BEING "prideful," two different concepts. There's nothing wrong with feeling pride. Feeling pride within yourself is considered a gift from God. Ecclesiastes 9:9 says, "Live joyfully with the wife whom thou goest all the days of the life of thy vanity, which he hath given thee under the sun, all the days of thy vanity: for that is thy portion in this life, and in thy labor which thou take under the sun." We're not in sin or should feel guilty for being proud of our work and in ourselves. It's when we are driven by it that it becomes a problem, when our happiness lies solely within it. Our identity cannot be based on exalting ourselves through our means. It will end up failing us. James 4:10, "Humble yourselves before the Lord, and He will lift you up." We go to God FIRST, and He will elevate us in His time. He will give us a portion of feeling proud of ourselves. He uses the word "portion" (like in Ecclesiastes) because it is just a PORTION of our happiness through Him. Remember, He gives us so much more than we could ever give ourselves.

We have to change our perspective of God, which only happens when we make a constant effort to get to know Him.

Of course, we will think we are made subject to bondage in Him if we haven't gotten to know Him on a deeper level. That's not a lack of love, that's lack of choosing to see Him differently. Has He not answered you when you needed Him because He's not there, or is it because you decided not fully to hear Him? He always answers me in the least way I expect Him to. When you don't know His character, it could be easy to miss. He uses manners least expected to prove Himself more. Think about it, when you expect an answer to come in a certain way, you don't fully appreciate it. If you find it in the most unpredictable and impossible of ways, it makes His glory fill you up even more than you could have imagined. John 10:10, "I have come that they may have life, and have it to the full." With God, nothing is mediocre. He's going to do it in a way that's going to make you feel the MOST love you could feel. Sometimes that means answering you in the least subtle ways expected.

We have to ask ourselves, "what lens am I looking through"? If I'm basing my expectation around doubt, then I'm potentially missing the good that He is doing already in my life. If I'm looking at Him through the lens of Him being a God of goodness, then that's what I will see. I'll give you an example through Scripture. Before I got to know Him on a deeper level, I would look at a verse in confusion such as Isaiah 45:7, "I form the light and create darkness: I make peace, and create evil: I the Lord do all these things." I would think, God created evil?! What the heck?! That's when I went to Him. He would always tell me with every Scripture, "It's all in how you look at it. I work for your good." "Okay, God, I'll look at it again." I wouldn't always get the answer right away. It took me studying other parts of the Bible to understand what certain Scriptures meant, especially that one entirely. I looked at the context of the theme of that Scripture. He was making a point toward the restoration (giving life back) to Jerusalem. He was saying no matter what evil happens; I am going to take control in due time, a better time. He wasn't saying He created evil to bring evil. The point He was making was that He was the Creator. He wanted to bring good out of evil and can regain control of it at any time. He created it, and it TURNED evil by free will. Do you see how easily your perspective can shift when you look at it through the right kind of lens? Don't let the enemy hand you the wrong lens.

1 John 4:7-8, "Beloved, let us love one another: for love is of God; and every one that loveth is born of God, and knoweth God. He that loveth not knoweth not God; for God is love." GOD IS LOVE. If we believe that, then we have to choose to see Him through that filter. What greater love could He possibly show than to send His son to die for us so He could take the keys of death and hell from Satan? We can now have access to eternal LIFE in heaven with Him. Not only after death but walking in His presence here on Earth through the gateway of the Holy Spirit that Jesus gave us when He died and rose again. He died for all, which INCLUDED the people He didn't agree with, the people who mocked Him, the people who KILLED Him, the religious, the unreligious, the atheist, the idolater.

There is no greater love to model after than the love of Jesus. He knows that we're going to fail at loving people, which is the whole point of having access to the Holy Spirit. All it takes is us making time for Him daily for His character to exude out of us to others. He's not looking to shame our cursed human nature but is looking to heal it through His love. He's looking to make us whole, so we can feel love and be love to others. We can fully achieve that through

Him, we just have to choose it. Colossians 3:14, "And above all these things, put on love which binds everything together in perfect harmony."

• CHAPTER 7 •

The Straight and Narrow

"There is a way that seems right to man, but the end thereof is death" (Prov. 14:12). On our own, we can go many different directions seeking life and benefit. The thing is, seeking desperately for self-growth without God's perspective causes us to be led by selfish intentions through our pride. Which is the perfect pathway that leads to self-destruction and the destruction of others. Each person can end up creating a pathway. How do we know the right way with so many different directions to choose from? God makes it easy for us. His pathway is considered "narrow" because of the simplicity of only having one way to go. His way brings life to ALL, not just one individual. He's looking to bring life to ALL. He doesn't say "narrow" to limit the people trying to seek life. He says it that way so we can understand that we only have to walk in one, simple direction. The perspective within that pathway contains so much clarity, joy, humility, fullness, and satisfaction. He wants to give us the best. The BEST means that there can only be one above all the rest. God only operates to give us the best. That means Satan can manipulate the rest, and his pathway only leads to death.

Okay, so in this chapter I'm going to dive pretty deep, and it will be a bit different from the rest of the book, but if I didn't speak the truth about the journey that God led me through, I would be holding back. I don't feel like God is telling me to hold back. You may want to brace yourself for this one because it is going to be quite a doozy.

Months ago, when God started to give me dreams and visions, He not only showed me events according to His will, He also unveiled to me horrible things that go along with the plan of the enemy. When I say "things," I mean dark things. A darkness that I didn't even know existed in this world. He led to me uncover the mappings of the enemy, opened my eyes to learn his ways, and his characteristics. Satan can't create; he only counterfeits what God creates. So, just like God works in patterns, the Devil does too as he tries to mimic and pervert. Keep in mind, Satan is NEVER original. He only steals. The dark, and honestly deep and depressing things that I have seen, really puzzled me. They started to make me feel hopeless. Remember, when your flesh makes you feel a certain way, you should always take your concerns and fears to God and rely on Him for clarity and comfort. I then asked Him, "God, why the heck are you showing me all these things"? He peacefully replied, "Sometimes, you have to understand the power of darkness, to understand the power you possess to overcome it." I was like, "WOW. Okay, God, show me what you will. I trust you."

I knew if I had remained in the place where I was at in my relationship with God before, I wouldn't be able to handle what I have discovered recently. I wasn't ready. I had to become more stable in Him before He could show me. God knows me; He knows my nature. I am a MAJOR researcher, almost in an unhealthy way. I make it my mission to find the truth. I don't like it when people are lied to or taken advantage of by deceptive practices or practitioners. I love to see people well, educated, empowered, and loved through Christ and in this world. I hate the way Satan has manipulated our culture into thinking anything less than that. God knew that the moment He gave me clues about certain things, I would relentlessly get to the bottom of the "why." I don't put it off either. You can ask my husband! There were many evenings when as soon as I got off work, I would spend hours reading and researching. There were moments where I had to tell myself to take a break to be a mom and wife. However, I knew this was a season where God was testing my limits, and I had to listen. Sometimes we go through a season of rest. Sometimes we go through an all-in, in-depth, submersed, soaking everything in kind of season.

When God communicates to me in dreams, I hear an evident and clear voice speaking to me. Many nights, it is around the same time in the middle of the night. God's words would be so loud they would wake me up from a deep sleep and make me jump up out of bed. I had to start keeping a notebook on my nightstand to write things down at night so that I wouldn't forget. I HIGHLY recommend you journal your thoughts and prayers. I also suggest dating the entries even down to the time. Remember, numbers are important to God as well. He uses them to confirm Himself through patterns. I would look up Biblical meanings to the numbers as well. But be careful as you research to not rely on the counterfeit understanding of numbers or numerology. Some of it is New Age Mysticism, and if you go down that path, you could end up deceived. I only use the Bible and Biblical commentary for the significance of numbers.

I was able to understand so much more and probably would have missed many things if I didn't search out the deeper meaning of repetitive numbers. I would have probably brushed many dreams off, thinking they were me, if I didn't journal the information to recognize the connecting patterns. Sometimes I could BLATANTLY recognize that it was the voice of God and other times, I had to study the Word in order to figure it out. There were many consecutive nights when the moment I laid my head down and closed my eyes to go to sleep, I would start seeing subtle shapes and pictures. Visions that I would have NEVER been able to come up with on my own since most of this stuff I didn't know existed. He showed me cultural, political, and geographical things. He even revealed to me things only understood in the astro and quantum physics world. I know I sound off my rocker and on shrooms or something, but just know I was in my right state of mind. I was in His state of mind. Before these dreams, I was very much a grounded realist who tended to lean more on the skeptical side of things.

I try to never approach a point of view in a biased sort of way so that I can be open to learning. The more He showed me, the deeper I dug. I even found myself reading 300 paged declassified FBI government documents uncovering some of the craziest undercover operations. Yes, they are out there online for all to see if you know what you're looking for topically. Let's just say that the Devil has infiltrated EVERYTHING because he's always looking to pervert what God creates. He's always looking to infiltrate systems of power. I honestly cannot comprehend why he still thinks he stands a chance of winning, but whatever.

Many of the revelations came to me after I started grieving and praying over what was surfacing with the whole Epstein case. I had been a passionate researcher in the anti-trafficking movements, so the details grieved me to the core. I felt something was much more in-depth (more than just the obvious). Shortly after I prayed, all hell broke loose (almost quite literally). The surface case in the public's eye was only a small piece of a giant puzzle of the enemy's plan that has been in operation for centuries. The more you dig, the more you discover a pattern linked to many internal groups. I was collecting information, and God connected the dots for me. It's hard to go into all the details because I could write an entire series of novels on everything I learned. However, I will recommend a good book you can read that will start you off on your journey to truth: The Killing of Uncle Sam by Rodney Howard Browne and Paul Williams. That book was just one of the books God led me to that helped me connect some dots on my visions and what I had researched. One of SO many books! If you can't receive the truth shared in that book, trust me, many books document the evidence about what is going on behind the scenes in our Nation and around the world. Much of it points back to the truths found in the Bible as well. I believe, The Killing of Uncle Sam is an excellent synopsis of what God was revealing to me.

There is a reason behind the sweeping corruption in government, finance, education, and medical institutions. Believe me, when I say, I was NO conspiracy theorist. I was far from it. I do not wear a tinfoil hat! LOL! However, I have so much research under my belt at this point, nothing would surprise me. The trends I started to see in the medical field alone where I am educated and work, was reason enough for me to start questioning things happening in our world. I've spent years educating people on the real truth in the medical field teaching them how to be smart, look for red flags, educate themselves, become their own health advocates, and to not be afraid to question or seek another opinion. We live in an evolving world. Some things that I did (based on FDA approval at that time) as a nurse when I first started, have now been taken out of practice because of potential harm. Because of experimentation, medical practices are in a constant state of change. Science is continually evolving. Along with that evolution, however, there's usually a lot of deceit coupled with it.

Much of what you can uncover is done by following the money trail. 1 Timothy 6:10 has a point when it says, "The love of money is the root of all evil." The truth will always surface, even if it takes years. Luke 8:17, "For there is nothing hidden that will not be disclosed and nothing concealed that will not be known or brought out into the open." You and I aren't idiots. We get gut feelings about things for a reason. If you don't have peace about something, DO NOT be afraid to question it. And loudly, if necessary! Give it to God first and let Him lead you to what He wants you to do about it. The enemy is trying to distract you while he uses people to plan out his schemes behind the scenes and in outlandish circumstances that are hard to believe for exactly that reason—to make you not believe.

I started to have random dreams about certain landmarks, specific cities, countries, and even numbers that lined up with different latitudinal and longitudinal placements. Yes, it was that specific. That's why I knew it had to have been from God. As I looked up the details to determine what they meant, I began to unravel way more than I bargained for in my quest for truth and what God was trying to teach me. The information I discovered would connect to specific points and places where elite groups would meet, where questionable events had taken place, and I found out they were all surrounded by common traits and themes. Though so many separate groups and names were involved, they all shared a related pattern. Those became red flags to me. I kept digging until I realized that many were, in fact, connected. When you dig to find out who these top affiliates are in large corporations, positions in government, banking, and educational systems and tie them to who they know and which organizations they are involved in, you realize you've unlocked some gross web of power and status. It's a web of deceit and destruction. Many of these groups are secretive and have one goal in mind: to gain power and control. These secret groups are interlocked within a plan that has trickled down for centuries. These world leaders are involved in the most mind-blowing practices you couldn't ever imagine. If you think Hitler was the only one with a sick agenda, believe me, he was not. In fact, reading his autobiography Mein Kampf, you'd be surprised to find out that much of his ideology wasn't conceived by him alone. He was the tool used by world leaders to bring it to life. His influence has infiltrated even beyond German borders.

Look into something called "Operation Paperclip," which is only one prime example.

Many of these groups perform sick ritualistic, demonic activities to advance and take advantage of the innocent. When I say ritualistic, I mean performing rituals, yes literal RITUALS to promote power. Rituals that stem back to ancient civilizations. Hang with me on this one. When you research into some of these groups, many of their symbols, ideals, belief systems, and connections can be traced back to a cult-like mindset involving sacrifices to false gods. I'm talking mainstream in the public's eye, except the public doesn't know it. A sick and disgusting net of deceit. The symbols that I was made aware of suddenly became things that I would see everywhere, every day. My eyes became open to seeing its existence in so many things. When I looked up to see what these symbols represented and the evil that hid behind them, I would be encompassed with a whole new world of emotions. I was sick to my stomach. It became evident that it was straight from Satan himself. No joke. I couldn't wrap my brain around the fact that the things

I would find out could be taking place. Why use such specific symbols in very specific patterns if you didn't have the original intention behind it?

When I thought it through, I realized if it's been happening for thousands of years, why the heck would it just go away? Satan is still here, tormenting and confusing people, so I knew his work still existed. His plan is to manipulate and destroy God's plan of life for us and many times, he uses people after power to fulfill his plan. It's even worse because it's intricately masked and hidden behind things we are involved in every day. I know I sound like a complete nut job at the moment, especially if you don't know me, but TRUST me I've done the research, and all I can tell you is pray and keep your eyes open to always look for God's truth.

Even before I started having visions, I made myself aware of what was going on, specifically within the medical industry. I am a registered nurse who has specialized in immunology. I work with autoimmune and immunodeficiency disorders. I've practiced and researched in this area for close to ten years. I, myself, have been diagnosed with autoimmune issues and started to see questionable trends within the industry years back. I devoted YEARS to finding answers through research and schooling. Believe me, when I say, there are many corrupt things infiltrated within our healthcare system to alter our health. I'm not saying everyone is suspect, and everyone in the industry is out to get you. Most people have good intentions. I'm saying that certain important people involved in the decision making have motives that are only looking out for them and their advancements within society. It's trickled down to deceive even the ones who are trying to do good.

You can trace the beginning of many pharmaceutical companies, "non-profit" organizations, and foundations (like Rockefeller Foundation, Rothschilds, etc.) to connections affiliated with the Nazi regime and their societal ideologies. Do you know that the chemical company (IG Farben) that supplied the gas for the gas chambers to Hitler branched off into three separate pharmaceutical companies post war? Bayer was one of them. I think it's no coincidence that Bayer owns many birth control medications as well as buying out Monsanto years back (the company that produces genetically modified seeds that have proven to alter and affect our fertility). The Rockefeller's had a lot to do with this transaction. Today, the Gates Foundation also financially supports Monsanto and partners with the Rockefeller Foundation to fund things like ID2021, Planned Parenthood, the NIH, and many vaccine companies such as Merck. Many of the vaccines that have been created through their financial support also have been linked to sterilization experimentation in communities in third world countries. There is a lot of evidence out there if you choose to open your eyes to it and do your research. These multi-billionaires influence much of our world today whether we realize it or not. I'm not trying to point my finger and blame the people when I say all these things. I'm very much aware that it's not the people who are necessarily evil, but the spiritual powers they are manipulated by.

You may, at this point, be asking why the heck did I just dump all that information on your lap? I had to give you a backstory to get to the point of this whole chapter. Some back story, huh? Ha! I believe that God is showing me these things (from what I gathered, many other people as well) because I honestly believe many of these issues are going to become evident more and more very soon. They already have in many ways if you know what to look for when questions arise. Satan uses people who pursue wealth and power to implement his plans. He has all throughout history, so why would he stop now? The Devil tries to control the minds of people, so he uses people in "control" and in authority to do so. He may even convince these people that they are doing things "for the betterment of mankind." Satan is the ultimate deceiver. He infiltrates anything and everything not being guided by God. He is getting more obvious with his infiltration. Heck, just look at the Disney Channel these days. A new children's show was introduced called the "Owl House" that is premised around a demonic underworld. Everything that is on that show is symbolic of something very real. You can look it up for yourself.

I believe God is showing people this so we can start identifying the real truth. God isn't calling us to stick our head in the sand. He's called us to be watchers. Biblical "watchmen" were responsible for warning the people when the enemy was rising against them to do them harm. He's calling us to turn evil into good, darkness into light. Be in the know but ask God to lead you into what you need to do. Being in the know is not premised around fear, it is so we can be led by Holy Spirit guidance to keep us from harm. He is the light that comes out of the darkness to bring hope. Many things will begin to surface, and it will start to get very confusing. If you believe anything in the Bible, you know that crazy things WILL manifest themselves. You have to be open to the possibility of them coming out in a way that's least expected. Satan is sly and conniving. He's a master of deceit, so you must be well informed and equipped so you can decipher what he will throw at you. Matthew 24:24 says, "For there shall arise false Christs, and false prophets, and shall show great signs and wonders; insomuch that, if it were possible, they shall deceive the very elect." The "elect" Jesus is referring to are those who believe they are following Christ. The false prophets represent a deceiving spirit that takes on a false Christ mindset. They are manipulated and used as puppets by Satan to act as a godlike figure to fool people. 1John 4:2-3 states, "Every spirit that confesseth not that Jesus Christ is come in the flesh is not of God: and this is that spirit of antichrist." Anyone who says Jesus did not come in the flesh to die for us and was raised to life is not of God. We must be in tune with the voice of the Holy Spirit.

He's going to protect us from deception, so we have nothing to fear.

Right now, as crazy as this sounds, on the History and Science Channels, they are obsessively talking about extraterrestrials and "ancient aliens." They claim that these beings made themselves known and have influenced ancient civilizations. It's not just on these channels either, I'm telling you, it's coming out more and more. Egyptians, according to the research and discoveries of the scientists on these channels, were the leading group influenced by these "extraterrestrial beings." Archeologists and Egyptologists have studied the hieroglyphics for years and have come up with this conclusion. For years, Hollywood and the media have played on these ideas of what was discovered. Many of the elite groups believe these ancient beliefs as well. Just investigate the history of the Masonic Lodge and the Illuminati and the well-known families who are involved. However, these concepts of "extraterrestrials" are slowly becoming a more mainstream belief. They are talking about it more since government projects and documents are being declassified and released. Look up "UFO" sightings in released FBI documents for yourself (specifically documents involving Roswell), if you don't believe me. They are saying on these channels that we come from these beings. They have also said that Jesus is a product of these "ancient aliens." The Vatican, believe it or not, is tied to this as well. Look into the "Lucifer Project" and the fact that the Vatican owns and operates the most advanced telescope located on Mount Graham in Arizona. They have an entire team of astrophysicists, who are more advanced than Nasa.

Now ask yourself, why the heck would they need that? We need to wake up and realize that more and more of this will start leaking out into society to manipulate the beliefs of Biblical understanding. Guy Consolmagno, one of the top astrophysicists at the Vatican and Director of the Vatican Observatory, was quoted a few years back saying, "Very soon the nations will look to aliens for their salvation," according to Tom Horn who has toured the facility and met Mr. Consolmagno himself. Say what? Crazy huh? As far out as this sounds, this is exactly what's being talked about prevalently. More and more evidence to prove their theories is explained to steer people away from the truth. According to a survey done by the Huffington Post in 2012, it stated that in the UK alone, just over 50% of the population believes in aliens over God.

Here's the kicker, I do believe in these "extraterrestrials," but not in the way that they are presenting their theories about them. I debated whether to address this because I didn't want to come off as a coo-coo bird. The thing is, these types of situations will surface again and again, and it will become very confusing for people. If it's not discussed and compared to the truth, God's truth, people will believe Satan's half-truths. Not being familiar with God's intentions and plan causes people to question and believe a lie. I think that the devil and his angels are behind many of these "UFO sightings." Yes, you read that right. The Bible said that Satan took a third of all angels with him. Many angels were created to be messengers and watchers of the Earth. However, they rebelled against God and were thrust to the Earth with Lucifer/Satan. Angels have a free will too, that's how Satan was able to take some with him. Many Scriptures detail how these messengers appear over and over. Hebrews 13:2 says, "Do not forget to show hospitality to strangers, for by so doing some people have shown hospitality to angels without knowing it." Angels can appear in human form without people even realizing it. Crazy thought, right? If God used angels as his messengers, I certainly believe Satan is also utilizing his fallen, dark angels to play out his strategies. Job 1:7 says, "Satan and his angels had appeared in front of the Lord and God had asked him where he had come from." Satan replied, "from going to and fro in the Earth and from walking up and down on it." 1 Peter 5:8 says, "Be sober, be watchful: your adversary the Devil, as a roaring lion, walks about, seeking whom he may devour." He and his angels have free reign to roam the Earth, appearing in the realms of the flesh deceiving people.

These beings HAVE influenced ancient civilizations, and they continue to impact our society today. These "ancient aliens" are what I believe the Bible refers to as Satan's fallen angels. He and his angels refer to themselves as "gods," and they have influenced culture and taught people the ways of mysticism and crooked pathways to exalt themselves above God. They are very active within our world. I do believe these "UFO" sightings have a lot to do with the demonic entities discussed in Scripture. His fallen angels are impacting our seen world. If you study the Bible closely, you will start to see why I believe that. The Bible talks about

God casting them to the waters, islands, wilderness, and mountains. Ezekiel 26:26, "all the princes of the sea." In verse 26:18, "the isles tremble in the day of thy fall." Zephaniah 2:11, "all the isles of the heathen." Hebrews 11:38, "men of whom the world was not worthy wandering in deserts and mountains and caves and holes in the ground." Genesis 14:10, "and the kings of Sodom and Gomorrah fled, and fell there; and they that remained fled to the mountain." If you study a lot on the term "princes" and lower case "kings," you'll find that the reference refers to the devil, his angels, and their demonic entities. Is it just coincidence that most of these "UFO sightings" are more prevalent in these areas of terrain?

Many people believe that Hitler himself was obsessed with these "extraterrestrials." If you investigate the things that Hitler was into, you might understand the reason he became so obsessed with the idea of establishing this so-called "perfect race." If you dig deep, you will find that he was beyond intrigued with the art of witchcraft and the occult. Winston Churchill in his memoir, The Gathering Storm, stated regarding Hitler, "He had conjured up the fearful idol of the all-devouring Moloch." Hitler mastered the art of the occult. The history of witchcraft is prevalent in Germany. In the 15th century, Germany was considered the witchcraft capital of the world. It was the birthplace of modern-day witches. It's also where the concept of Halloween originated. Hitler was involved with an occult called "The Thule Society," formed shortly after WWI that stemmed from ancient ideologies and beliefs. These ideologies were adopted by Hitler and became formally known as the Nazi Party. Many of Hitler's top men attended the occult meetings and believed and submitted to them whole-heartedly. Because of Hitler's grandiose delusions, the leader of the occult (Dietrich Eckart) saw Hitler as his new spokesperson for the group. He was intrigued and learned much about witchcraft, practicing it entirely because it gave him "power." His ritualistic practices empowered him to master the art of manipulating the mindsets of the people so he could build his new nation. He took on the spirit of Satan and the antichrist himself.

Hitler was obsessed with ancient Egyptian beliefs and took on a pharaoh like persona. He had plans to build an entire empire called "Germania" modeled after ancient Egyptian and Babylonian architecture. He was also obsessed with breeding people (Lebensborn Program) and experimenting with their DNA in order to achieve his perceived "pure race." Just a basic Google search of the "Thule Society" can give you all the info you need on that. He was determined to have his "thousand-year Reich" continued to be passed on even beyond his years. In fact, newly released FBI documents show evidence that Hitler faked his death and escaped to South America. He was determined to continue his legacy, and nothing was going to stand in his way. His rituals, I believe, summoned demonic entities. Documents shown on an episode of "Nazi Secret Files" on the American Heroes Channel, explained how Hitler was being manipulated by a "higher power" and would see beings described as tall with blonde hair and blue eyes. There are tons of leaked documents and reports that claim this as well if you start searching for them. Edward Snowden was one of many who leaked out knowledge from the NSA, which stated that Hitler was being led by a race of "tall white men." That would make sense of his obsession with blond hair and blue eyes when he didn't have those traits. It would also be logical to believe those reports because Hitler's foundation of the entire Nazi party was based on the beliefs that the Thule Society had about the Aryan race. There's also a reason why many of these "UFO" sightings happened just shortly after WW2 ended. Lord knows what kind of deal Hitler made to try to win the war. It may explain why there was a mass sacrifice of Jews as well. If you look up the history and beliefs of this "Nordic race" and the "Thule Society," they blame the Jews for destroying the world. Wouldn't that sound exactly like something coming from Satan? Biblical history can attest to why Satan was against the Jews. He hates every person God has chosen for Himself.

So why did I even bring any of that up? Because I believe it is crucial. Believe it or not, there are many influential people with similar ideologies today that the Devil has manipulated into operating in these same behaviors and beliefs. These "entities" are still around influencing many people. It would be naive to believe that Satan doesn't use people in power. The Bible is proof of that fact with people like Pharaoh and King Nebuchadnezzar to name a couple. You will soon find more and more of this "alien" talk start to leak out. I think it is imperative to understand what these beings are. You will also see it related to "artificial intelligence" as well. That's a whole other thing that I believe that the Devil is using to confuse people into thinking that "merging" with such intelligence is for the "betterment of society." Research more into this yourself. It's absolutely mind boggling. As crazy as it sounds, this deception is everywhere, and it's only just beginning to confuse the generations. We have to establish a strong sense of stability in the truth according to the Word of God. Otherwise, we may get steered in the wrong direction.

The devil works against the truth, twisting it at just the right points for you to believe his lie. How else do you think he will try to convince people to follow him? He works WITH the truth to pervert it ever so slightly to fit his desires. He uses fear to lure people toward a false sense of "safety." He uses the Bible in many ways. Ezekiel 13:6 says, "They have seen vanity and lying divination, saying, the Lord saith: and the Lord hath not sent them: and they have made others to hope that they would confirm the word." He gives people partial truth to confuse them. If you're not careful and grounded in the Word of God and your faith, you might easily become deceived as well. When I started unraveling his patterns, I, too, had moments of confusion. One Scripture to keep in mind is 1 Corinthians 14:33, "For God is not a God of confusion but of peace." If you get an ick feeling in the pit of your stomach and it seems off, most likely, it's not God. It is CRUCIAL for you to get grounded in the Truth (the Bible and the voice of the Holy Spirit). If not, you WILL get confused. While he is NOT more powerful than God, we must realize Satan is real and powerful. However, we also have to know we are MORE powerful when we are equipped with the foundation of truth, THE Truth, God's Word.

I believe that's EXACTLY why God tests us in many ways. It's so we can tell the difference between what's Him and what isn't Him. The Parables of Jesus are excellent examples of teaching us how to understand and hear the voice of God. One of the reasons why the Bible can sometimes speak in hard to understand Parables is to inspire us to learn how to lean into His voice. In Matthew 13:11, Jesus explains to the disciples why He uses Parables. "Because it is given unto you to know the mysteries of the kingdom of heaven, but to them, it is not given." Meaning, it's given freely to those who seek after the voice of the Father. Those who don't diligently spend time with Him won't be able to understand His intentions and will misinterpret Scripture.

You have to learn how He speaks to you individually. For me, I also had to learn how to STUDY the Bible, and not just read it. You must make it your go-to lifeline because that's what the Bible should be. A GREAT podcast and YouTube Channel to listen to is called "The Bible Project." These guys do a fantastic job explaining the text and meaning of different themes throughout the Bible. It's a perfect starting point for you. Heck, it's a great any point for you. As God showed me all these crazy demonic things, I couldn't help but be disturbed, even though I couldn't understand why. Some of the rituals involved spells and human sacrifice, which are straight out of the Old Testament pagan sacrifices. Yes, people, then and now, even sacrifice children.

The Epstein case was just a small glimpse into what takes place in human trafficking and sacrifice. There's a reason why he flew out elite groups of powerful people to a private island fully equipped with a freaky temple and altar. The elites have a track record of meeting secretly and performing odd behavior. A modern-day example of odd and private meetings includes the annual Bilderberg Meeting. Bohemian Grove is another modern-day meeting place for people from high places of authority to gather. There's nothing more disturbing than seeing past presidents and government officials participating in a ceremony dedicated to the pagan deity Moloch (research the documentary "Dark Secrets: Inside Bohemian Grove"). Many government officials have openly stated they are proud members before this documentary was released. According to the National Park Services website, the UN was established north of San Francisco in Muir Woods after a memorial tribute to Franklin D. Roosevelt. This also happens to be the place where the Bohemian Grove ceremonies take place. Seems like a very odd coincidence don't you think? Leviticus 18:21 says, "Thou shalt not let any of thy seed pass through the fire to Moloch, neither shalt thou profane the name of thy God: I am the Lord." Moloch sacrifices were children.

As I uncovered a lot of this and read what the ancient people were doing in the Old Testament, God showed me bit by bit why people do this. It wasn't that they were trying to kill their kids (not in their manipulated mind anyway). They thought they were handing their children over into an after-life to give them power. It was also to obtain power themselves and prosperity, which is what Satan convinced them would result.

Now you may ask, why the heck would Satan do that? You see, Satan is considered "dead" in the eyes of God. Since his destiny is the Lake of Fire, eternal damnation, Satan, who loves to destroy eternal life with God, wants to kill people and prevent them from eternal life in heaven through faith in Jesus Christ. He doesn't care about babies or children or families. He is death, and his desire for death is never satisfied. That's what he and his angels were trying to do with the Egyptians and other ancient civilizations. They were always trying to access through a crooked pathway, trying to be exalted above God. The Tower of Babel is a prime example of it. Just like Lucifer, they were trying to rise above God. They were trying to achieve god-like power. God confused and dispersed the people at the Tower of Babel so they would not end up misusing the power achieved on their own that would ultimately lead to their destruction. God freely gives His wisdom to those who humbly ask, which always brings life. You become one with Him as you become more like Christ. When you try to access knowledge on your own, it leads to the destruction of yourself and others. Hitler was the perfect post Biblical history example of this. You see, we can't handle all access to knowledge without God because we aren't able to see how He sees. Just look at where all the ancient cultures ended. They either mysteriously disappeared or crumbled. Their quest for knowledge and power led to destruction, which is what will ultimately happen to Satan.

Even the people whose intent is for the "betterment of society," who pursue knowledge without being led by God, will ultimately result in creating further problems. I see this often within the medical field. Everyone is trying to solve the issues of society. The thing is, they stay behind the trail of consequences from their mistakes by trying to handle it on their own without God's direction. "Solutions" create more problems to solve until it ultimately leads to more destruction. That is why it is especially important to not be driven by fear, which leads us to solve problems on our own without the help of God. Just like in the Garden. Fear and pride drive us to "eat of the wrong fruit." When we eat the fruit of knowledge with our own pride it leads us to harm.

God, on the other hand, teaches us to become Christ-like through love, in a sustainable way that keeps us and others from harm. Satan leads people to destruction through self-exaltation. God's way is for the benefit of ALL. Satan's way is for the benefit of SELF only.

Satan also used people to build altars to him, just like God's people did to Him. If you research the world's temples, pyramids, altars, and stone patterns, they all line up with what's called electromagnetic lines. They are so intricate and detailed, even astronomically lining up down to an exact degree of measurement. Just research into the Great Pyramid alone, and you will be mind-blown. There's a reason why the patterns of Egypt's pyramids and hieroglyphics match patterns and symbols with civilizations on the other side of the world like the Mayans in Mexico. Ezekiel 29:12, "I will scatter the Egyptians among the nations, and will disperse them through the countries." Even before the flood, I believe, these people were in one place being taught these things by the Devil and his fallen angels. Genesis 6, Job 1:6, Jude 6, 2 Corinthians 4:4 and 12:7, among many other references, refer to their interactions with humans. The Egyptians seemed to be the ones who were most influenced throughout the Old Testament and also within secular historical data. If you study Scripture in the Old Testament about the Egyptians, you will see that they were masters at magic and mysticism. It was because they were influenced by the teachings of the Devil and his fallen angels, who referred to themselves as deities and gods.

The Devil was teaching them because he was trying to build an army against God. He was, and is now, always trying to find ways to re-access paradise and infiltrate the high places of God. Which is why Scriptures like 2 Kings 21:3 and 4 discuss high places of the Lord being corrupted and replaced by the high places dedicated to pagan gods. References to "high places" in the Bible are altars and spiritual access points like temples where people offered worship to false gods. Remember, Jesus had not yet been made the perfect sacrifice to give them a permanent pathway. And for many of those who don't believe in Jesus today, those corrupted pathways are still trying to be utilized. There were many forms of altars. Pyramids, stones, mountains, even trees were used as altars. These altars are a place of worship where people believe they can be transformed into a higher and more powerful being. It was a way for them to become "altered." However, many were transforming while dedicating their souls and spirits to the devil and his schemes. These altars acted as portal spots and gateways for them to access the knowledge of the "gods." Again, it all goes back to the Tree of Knowledge of Good and Evil in the Garden. That's precisely what the devil was continuing to do. He was trying to use people to exalt themselves above God selfishly and to lead them to destruction. All of these portals into the spiritual realm, in the form of temples and altars, were crooked pathways to access paradise. Isaiah 59:8, "They do not know the way of peace, and there is no justice in their tracks; they have made their paths crooked, whoever treads on them does not know peace."

One thing Satan has become obsessed with is mimicking and killing God's seed. It was brought on by the curse when they ignored the voice of God in the Garden. He is adamant about bringing corruption and manipulation to the seed. Remember when I said what happens in the spiritual is reflected of the natural? Well, we are God's seed both in the spiritual AND in the natural. He created us in His image and from His patterns. The patterns of DNA that He created in our cells are what I believe to be considered as the seed of God in the natural realm. DNA contains the blueprint of our cellular makeup. Modern science makes discoveries all the time about how intricate and marvelous the patterns of our DNA genuinely are. The devil works to bring corruption in the spiritual, which reflects directly into the natural. He brings sickness to us by affecting our DNA.

Do you want to know the first thing that living viral and bacterial organisms do in us? They swim around with intent and purpose, looking for DNA to cling to for corruption. They go directly to it, latch on, manipulate the pattern of the DNA, and replicate the new altered state of it. If that isn't a direct reflection of Satan maneuvering in our body, I don't know what is. Nothing screams Satan more than an annoying little disgusting virus. Everything Satan does brings destruction and corruption to the life that God has bestowed on and in us. Through Jesus, God undid the patterns Satan used to corrupt everything in the world and humanity. We receive His finished work by realizing the battle begins in the Spiritual realm. Once received, His healing reflects in the natural.

Knowing what I know about the body and science, it has helped me to realize that the unseen realm impacts and affects our natural bodies. I believe that God physically moves as an unseen force that scientists call the "God particle" (that dark unseen matter mentioned in Chapter 2), which holds our cells together. His presence and His frequencies within what we cannot see, can move more in water, because of the more potent magnetic and electrical force in its properties. I believe that's why His Holy Spirit is symbolic of water many times. Well, I think it's no coincidence that 92% of what travels in our blood vessels (which feeds our cells) is water. Scientists at the Helmholtz-Zentrum Dresden-Rossendorf (HZDR) have discovered that water molecules ravel within the dark matter among the spirals of our DNA. Water has the capability of carrying strong frequencies of the unseen realm. That could also be one of the reasons why Leviticus 17:14 says, "the life of every creature is its blood; anyone who eats it must be cut off." The life source of a creature is within the blood. Life flows within the blood. If we lose too much blood, we die. It supplies our body with the necessary nutrients and oxygen needed to survive. Just as the blood gives life by things flowing in it, it can also bring corruption by the manipulated particles in it as well. There are so many hidden reasons why God gave rules for man to follow when it came to animal sacrifices. Scripture states that people were not to take part in drinking the blood of the sacrifice. I will share why in a second.

He showed me that our blood cells represent our natural existence here on Earth. His force that is so prevalent in water moving alongside our cells is the symbol of His Spirit connected to us here on Earth. That's why I believe the Bible always references Him "entering into our hearts." Our hearts are pumps that pump our life (blood) throughout our being. Proverbs 4:23, "Keep thy heart with all diligence; for out of it are the issues of life." References to the heart of man also refer to the spirit of man, the very center point of who we are in Christ. I love how God manifests Himself in the seen and unseen realm. God is science.

The animal sacrifices in the Old Testament were examples of atoning work. Listening to God's voice helped me understand why certain sacrifices were performed. Okay, when I go into all this, please keep in mind this is what I believe God is showing me. I cannot 100% prove it to you, but when I explain it, the light may come on for you too. Sometimes things in the Bible don't make sense until the pieces come together. Let me see if I can help. There is a reason for everything, multiple reasons too. God works in many mysterious ways.

Anytime there's death involved, I always have to look for the reason why. Leviticus goes over all the rules of animal sacrifice and why it was needed. Rules like which animals to use for each specific sin and reason. As mentioned over and over throughout this book, there's a purpose for everything. Anytime the Levites had to make animal sacrifices, it was because they were undoing what Satan had convinced the rest of the Israelites to do when they committed sins or made sacrifices to false gods. You see, anytime they would perform these sacrifices upon the altars ("high places") and make things "pass through the fire," they would eat the meat. They were undoing the sacrifices made by the corrupted previous sacrifices influenced by Satan. However, whenever they were reversing the sins of their behaviors or the past sacrifice, they had to make the new sacrifice clean. They couldn't eat the new sacrifice without salting the meat before they cooked it. Salt draws the blood and water out of the meat, acting as a purification process. Here in Louisiana, we do what is called "purging the crawfish" before we boil them. We pour tons of salt in the pot of water where they're sitting. The reason why we have done this over the decades is to detox them from what they consumed. They are bottom feeders that consume disgusting toxins. The salt causes them to vomit out the nasties (sorry for the gross visual). Salt is a "purger." It's cleansing. There's even a Salt Covenant of God in the Old Testament that was symbolic of the promise of the love of God. The salt represented the purging of sin with the love of God. I also think that is why we are called "salt of the Earth" in the New Testament, we act as purifiers in love throughout the world.

Then there's the leavened and unleavened bread. Want to know the difference? There is a spiritual significance symbolizing sin, but there is also a natural realm significance as well. God forbids the Israelites from eating leavened bread. There's always a big reason behind why God forbids something. Well, ancient civilizations would perform rituals of human sacrifice, roast the meat, and eat it, and use the leftover blood and ash to make the bread (Isaiah 44:19). How flipping disgusting! They would also take the residue of the remains and make "graven idols" of themselves to worship (Isaiah 44:17). At first, I thought, surely, I misread this. I read other references as I researched further and sure enough, blood was and is used to perform most spells in witchcraft. I don't want to give you references because of the heaviness attached, but just a basic Google search can give you more than enough evidence of that fact. I believe this is one-way Satan goes after God's seed (us) in the natural. He convinces these people he will offer them power and riches by dedicating and sacrificing their blood to him. They are deceived into thinking that they are doing this to royal deities who can provide them protection and power.

Instead, the devil manipulates and corrupts their physical DNA. Want to know how? When you eat meat and blood that hasn't been purified and cooked thoroughly, you can take on the DNA that travels through bacteria and microscopic organisms. The DNA then replicates itself over and over, which can, in turn, alter your DNA. The DNA of living organisms is within each one of their cells. If not destroyed, it can mix with those who eat it. Maybe that's why people started to pray over their food?? Side note, that's probably why God refers to man and wife as "one flesh" when they become married (use your imagination). That's why it is so important to keep sacred things sacred. That also might be the reason behind why they considered the woman "unclean" in Biblical times during her menstrual cycle and during the bleeding that occurs postpartum. Science has discovered that DNA from the fetus is leftover in the mother's blood for up to 6-8 weeks after birth. Crazy huh?

Research the effects of mixing DNA between organisms. I know this all sounds super gross, but I have a point to all this insane madness. Sometimes we have to be made aware of certain truths (no matter how grotesque) to understand why we have to do the things we do. It's why we must do certain things to keep safe. It was why God's instructions were so precise. Maybe that explains all the "pure" lineage list Scriptures in the Bible because of all the crazy unclean DNA and flesh swapping that was going on! He was listing it all out to show that God's seed was pure both spiritually AND naturally.

There is one disturbing example that takes place in modern medicine. We can simply investigate vaccine production alone. New technology and research have started to use and experiment with gene editing proteins in these vaccines. Their purpose is to reprogram our genes to adapt and respond better against foreign toxins and diseases. They basically want to manipulate the structure of our DNA for "our benefit." This has proved to be potentially detrimental to our health. I cannot make this stuff up. Another disturbing component within many vaccines such as the chickenpox, shingles, Varicella, DTaP, the MMR, Hep A, and the rabies are all made by growing viruses on the cells of aborted fetuses (stem cells). The vaccine list that uses aborted fetal cells is also continuing to grow. They use fetal cells because of the increased stability to be transferred within our immune system to cause activation. The fetal cells have been more effective when it comes to growing and sustaining the viruses on them. Though much of the DNA is destroyed during the process, there are still leftover fragmented DNA that have the ability to affect the host body's DNA. Just one single amino acid change can potentially affect the development of sex chromosomes. In 1991, scientists were able to transform female mice embryo to male by simply inserting one single SRY gene. The SRY gene is found on the Y chromosome and is the sex-determining gene. When studying the effects of stem cell transplantation, researchers also found that the SYR gene from the donor DNA was present in the subject that was receiving the stem cell transplant proving that it was capable of being transferred over from subject to subject.

There are also enhancers in the dark matter of our DNA that could also be transferred. If the genes themselves don't transfer over, these enhancers within the dark matter may. These enhancers can affect sex development in unborn babies and infants as well as older kids. Professor Andrew Sinclair at the University of Melbourne states, "If these enhancers that control testis genes are disrupted in any way, it may lead to a baby being born with a disorder of sex development." His research partner Brittany Croft also stated, "human sex reversal is caused by gain or loss of the vital enhancers that regulate our sex genes." Could this be one reason that we have such a gender identity crisis in our society now? We just never know.

By saying all this, I'm certainly not claiming that getting vaccinated with vaccines that use this technology is a sin. Not in the least bit. I'm also not trying to bring shame to the those who have chosen to be vaccinated. If these facts concern you, bring them to God. He knows the intent behind the things that we do. He even knows the intent behind the vaccine creators. However, I do believe that Satan has manipulated the industry into using techniques that can potentially bring us harm. He's manipulated multiple industries. It all comes down to trying to solve problems and increasing knowledge on our own without God. Satan still influences people in the same ways he did in the Bible. His plan never changed. Knowing the truths behind these things is super important for us in order to pray against their harm.

I do also want to point out another fact about aborted fetuses because many do not know this. Once the mom decides to abort, the fetus becomes the property of either the state or the facility. They keep the fetus alive as long as they can to harvest cells and organs to be sold on the black market, whether for "research" or to whomever to do whatever. There are MANY deceptions out there about abortions. Just the fact that mothers are lied to about the fetus not feeling the procedure is a load of crap. A baby's heartbeat starts between the fourth and fifth week. Pain receptors are developed just before twelve weeks. And most abortions take place after this mark of time. If we consider the end of our life to be the moment our heart stops, shouldn't we consider the start of life when the heart starts? Sisters, I know you feel it's your body, your choice, and your life, but please consider the life of the ones who don't have a choice and who can't speak out. There are many other options, and you can still have the freedom to choose those. God restores, and He makes a way when there is no way, even in the most incomprehensible circumstances. He protects those who protect the innocent. Sorry for the long side tangent, but I had to get that off my chest. I've dedicated lots of research into the Pro-Life and Pro-Choice movements all because I wanted to understand both sides. I also want to state that He restores and redeems people after the abortion has already taken place as well. He knows the intent of your heart.

With that said, let's get back to Biblical history. When all these pagan rituals were taking place, they were performing them in locations that were considered holy unto God. It was Satan's way to steal and claim dominion. That's why the Levites were called back to the holy places to perform a reverse sacrifice unto the Lord to make it clean again. Not with human sacrifice, but with animals. God's original intention was not to kill any living creature until He had to use

Jesus to undo what Satan did. He had to reverse the sacrifice with life for a life. I think that's why God tested Abraham when He told him to sacrifice his son Isaac. God knew the whole time He wouldn't require the life of Isaac. Abraham trusted that God would spare his son's life either way, whether it was in the world or the eternal. The point was Abraham believed. God was only using it as a test to promise to spare the rest of Abraham's "seed" lineage into life eternal. God knew that Abraham grew up around these pagan rituals, and it was a test to see if he would offer up his seed, just like the pagans did to their gods. He was making it a point that in saving Isaac's life, He didn't come to destroy a life like Satan does, but to save a life. It was God's way of saying, "You see, that's what separates Me from other gods. They require death, but I spare and bring life when you bring your heart to me. My love is given freely." It was one of the biggest indicators to Abraham that He was the one TRUE God.

Sure, can many of these other "god" followers feel happy and temporarily secure? Yes, but only for a short while. The deals the devil makes, as well as other pagan gods (fallen angels), always require taking something away from people. Keep in mind, the devil even uses human pride as a form of a god. Self-exaltation may have temporary satisfaction, but it ultimately has eternal destruction. However, with Yahweh, He comes to give life and eternal riches freely to those who choose Jesus Christ as Lord and Savior.

Sometimes it takes uncovering the ugly to appreciate the beautiful. Sometimes it takes digging up the ENTIRE truth to make a wise decision. I hope and pray you are made aware of some of these truths and look to the one main Truth that saves, Jesus. It's better to believe even a smidgen of the possibility that the power of the darkness exists, so when the appointed times come for them to manifest themselves, you're not caught off guard. That's what Scriptures mean when they say to be "ready." Don't let the enemy convince you to keep your blindfold intact. You're only as blind as you want to be. John 12:40, "He has blinded their eyes and hardened their heart, lest they see with their eyes, and understand with their heart, and turn, and I would heal them."

Don't let the devil convince you that you are lacking anything, even when it comes to the knowledge of the world. God will reveal things to you through Him, the right and safe way. That's what He did with me. He gave me revelations to even the hard truths, but He paired them with a hope and a solution. Daniel 2:20, "He gives wisdom to the wise and knowledge to those who have understanding. He reveals deep and secret things; He knows what is in the darkness, and light dwells with Him." You want to feel empowered, fulfilled, loved, and have the clarity for things you don't understand? He'll give that to you. When I kept seeking God, He revealed "mysteries of the heavens" I didn't even know existed. I didn't have to travel to these ancient portal sites to receive it. God sent Jesus to us to be a "portal"/gate to access His presence and everything through Him. He is the straight gate to enter God's throne room. Matthew 13:24, "Enter in at the straight gate: for wide is the gate, and broad is the way that leads to destruction." The Lord promises in Isaiah 45:2, "I will go before thee and make the crooked places straight." Proverbs 3:6, "In all your ways acknowledge Him, and He will make your paths straight." David cried out to God in Psalms 5:8, "Lead me, O Lord, in thy righteousness because of mine enemies; make thy way straight before my face." God fulfilled His promise to David by sending Jesus to be the straight pathway to gain access into His presence. It doesn't require a physical temple that lies on an electrical charged energy hot spot, either. Acts 7:48, "The most High dwells not in temples made with hands." Verse 55 says, "But he being full of the Holy Ghost, looked up steadfastly into heaven, and saw the glory of God and Jesus standing on the right hand of God." We have access to His throne room through Jesus, and the Holy Spirit will help us get there. He's available to everyone who accepts Him. Don't let the lies convince you that you don't have access to God's wisdom. Don't let the ideas of the culture and the crazy documentaries on the History Channel make you feel that you need to travel abroad to soak up the "energy of the gods." You have ALL you need through Him. He lacks nothing; therefore, we lack nothing. 2 Peter 1:3, "He has given us ALL THINGS that pertain to life and godliness."

So, stay on the straight pathway with Him. He loves you so much and He will lead you in life to the wonderful plans He has for you and those you bring to heaven with you.

• CHAPTER 8 •

Spiritual Authority

Since I was little, I have always had dreams. But I have to admit, most nights, as a child, I had nightmares. I used to be so afraid to go to sleep at night. Even as a child, I was always sensitive to the unseen. I would feel things around me that I couldn't explain. Sometimes I would cry to my mom before bed because I didn't want to go to sleep. It was then when she taught me an authoritative Scripture that unknowingly at the time became the foundation of my security today. 2 Timothy 1:7, "For God has not given us a spirit of fear, but of power, love, and a sound mind." I would say that Scripture out loud every night before bed. For years I use to think it didn't work because I would still have nightmares. But it would comfort me enough to go to sleep even though bad dreams might still come. It wasn't until I got older that I realized how those nightmares would serve as a tool in building a stronger foundation of faith and spiritual authority. As I worked through those times of fear with God's Word, I learned how to practice declaring the truth about the security that was promised to me, even when I didn't fully understand it at the time. I realize now, that if praying that Scripture would have taken those nightmares away, I wouldn't be able to face some of the scariest things with ease as I do now. I needed to strengthen my spiritual armor. I needed to see the darkness exposed to learn how to overcome it. After years of praying that Scripture, it eventually gave me a different perspective on what I once defined as scary. I recognized that I had a stabilizing peace through it all that kept me from being affected, which instilled confidence in me that made me feel I could face anything. Slowly, but surely, I was taking spiritual authority over darkness and evil attacking my life.

Don't get me wrong; I still have to battle thoughts of doubt and fear. Just being a protective mom of three precious kids causes me to have anxiety. God knows that our first reaction is to doubt and to look for the harm in situations. Our natural response is to sense danger so that we can protect ourselves and our loved ones. The thing that God looks at is what we will do next. Will we give focus to the fear, or will we trust in Him for our protection? It's about creating an ongoing habit of relying on Him. In that, He will show you what you are capable of and what His protection provides. That is what keeps me secure. Being adamant about studying Scripture and making myself hungry to understand it is when He started bringing growth to my faith and confidence in His protection.

I was lying in bed one night, in complete quiet and darkness, asking Jesus to show Himself to me. When you approach Him with a genuine desire to feel His presence, and earnestly look for Him, He will reveal Himself in the most beautiful ways. At this point, He had made me feel so loved and comforted that I longed for it daily. I honestly have never felt so close to Him before. As I was lying there, I began to see visions of beautiful colors like the colors within our Milky Way Galaxy. Vapor-like images were floating as if they were graceful butterflies swimming slowly underwater. Yes, swimming, blue and green, vapor butterflies. I know that sounds weird and far out there, but that's the best way I can describe it. Anytime I see visions, that's how they always begin. It's as if I am breaking through a barrier full of floating angels in space or something.

Once those cleared away, I began to see the silhouette of the face of Jesus. His face then morphed into a full-body silhouette walking toward me. At this point in the night, my kids were still awake. They were loud and obnoxious, and it became a distraction to me. Once I gave focus to what was around me, my frustration grew. My vision started to get blurry, and it was as if a wall was placed right in front of Jesus. He became hidden. In my frustration, I prayed, "Jesus, please, show yourself to me again. I just want to see you. Help me to see you again. Why did you go away"? His still small voice inside said, "I'm right here. I'm always right here." In some way, I understood an entire conversation He was communicating to me. He explained to me that what you give more focus becomes what you will see. "As long as you are in your physical body, only seeing the physical realm in front of you, you will always be tempted to doubt. The thing is, I'm always here. I never went away. Your focus on the things around you is what put the wall there, not Me. You just have to look past what you SEE is there and believe in what you KNOW is there with you that you cannot see. That's when you will see Me. When you believe I am here, press in further, and you will find Me. I didn't go anywhere." Right then, I understood what Peter went through as he walked on water toward Jesus. Jesus was always there. The moment Peter took his eyes off Jesus and gave focus to the environment around him, that's when fear and doubt made him sink. When we give more attention to our surroundings, to the things that bring us fear, we give it power over our lives. Romans 8:13 says, "For if you live according to the flesh you will die, but if by the Spirit you put to death the deeds of the body, you will live."

After this vision, I was determined to practice seeking and relying on Jesus beyond what the physical tries to convince me to believe. The reason I didn't walk in total security and trust in Jesus before is that I wasn't seeking Him daily like I am now. The more I give focus to Him, the more I will see that He is here with me all the time. You may ask, "Then why do Christians still get hurt"? I get it. I used to ask the same thing. Here's a clue, we live in a fallen world. But the thing is, the moment we stop giving Jesus our focus, the more room we leave open for Satan to come in and try to harm us. It's not that Jesus doesn't protect us; it's because we put a block on Him when we ignore Him. We get so caught up in trying to meet our own needs; we drift away from what is pleasing to God. His being "pleased" doesn't mean that He selfishly wants us not to be happy and for us to become slaves to His rules. Like mentioned before, His ways are established to protect us and to provide for us beyond what we could ever expect or even deserve. He wants to give us more than what we can give ourselves. One thing He has given us is spiritual authority over all the works of the enemy. Luke 10:19, Jesus is talking here, "Behold, I give unto you power (some versions say, authority) to tread on serpents and scorpions, and over all the power of the enemy: and nothing shall by any means hurt you."

We all know that we mess up and ignore the Father daily. We have to understand; when we ignore His direction, we fall into the traps of the enemy's destruction. Often, for us to walk in the full authority of what He has given us, we must first come to Him with a repentant heart to purify ourselves so we can break the strongholds of the enemy. Joshua 7:13

says, "Sanctify yourselves against tomorrow. There is an accursed thing in the midst of thee, O Israel: thou cannot stand before thine enemies, until ye take away the accursed thing from among you." The tribes of Israel could not stand strong in battle because they had not made themselves pure (humble and repentant) before the Lord. Why? You can't go into battle with half of your armor or chinks in that armor. You can't go into battle with your plan without adequately being prepared for what you are facing. Jesus FULLY preps us for action. We have to get rid of our pride and allow Him to make us ready to stand firmly secured in Him. Ephesians 6:13, "Wherefore take unto you the whole armor of God, that ye may be able to withstand in the evil day, and having done all, to stand."

Another dream I had recently was God's way of telling me that I needed to be conscientious of protecting myself. As long as we live in a cursed and fallen world (until the day He renews it), we have to be mindful to put on our spiritual armor daily. In my dream, I was in a parking lot of a local drugstore with my three kids. They were all playing and riding their bikes in the parking lot. My middle son always likes to play outside without shoes and a shirt. He's such a country boy. The kid hates shoes. Anyways, he was riding his bike, and suddenly, he face-planted into the concrete and scuffed his whole body up. I fussed at him while I was urgently racing to his rescue. I kept telling him over and over, "Karter, you have to wear protection! You can't forget to put on protection"! I then looked over at the street just beyond the parking lot. Three dark figures were staring at us. One of them pointed directly at me. I grabbed the kids and said, "We have to go home right now." I woke up right after. God told me that this was a sign never to leave your house without spiritual protection. We seek shelter in His home in the Spirit. We have to daily learn to lean on His promises, believing and declaring them, and wearing our spiritual armor before we are faced with an attack.

He said, "The enemy is always trying to find an opportunity to attack you. The moment you block me or lose trust in me, you open a window of opportunity for the attack to come." So, I asked God, "Okay, I get it. How do I spiritually protect myself"? I was led to search out Scriptures to pray and declare over my family and me every day. I try to make it a point to proclaim these Scriptures before doing anything else during my day. I don't do that because I live in fear. It's quite the opposite. The enemy cannot withstand the Word of God. It makes the devil and his minions quiver. They may not be intimidated by my word, but they sure as heck will be fearful of what the Word of the Lord has to say. His Word is your authority. Once you practice saying Scriptures over your life, you will soon be able to see the point of why it is so important for you to do it. As I came to Him in prayer one night trying to look for Scriptures to utilize, I randomly opened my Bible to the book of Psalms. The top of my page said, "prayers of David." When I saw those words, it was like I knew instantly that's what I had to read and declare.

A few days prior, I had bought a small pocket notebook to write down Scriptures that I felt led to note. I started reading, and the moment a verse would strike a strong response in me, I would write it down. There was no order I was following. I just copied what stood out to my spirit. Before I knew it, I filled up seven pages. I didn't realize it was seven pages until I counted. It served as another little reminder that God was in the lead. He likes to show Himself in even the smallest of ways. Though it may be long, I want to give you what God gave me from the Psalms so you can read them in one paragraph:

"Psalms 19:13 & 14, Keep back thy servant also from presumptuous sins; let them not have dominion over me: then shall I be upright and I shall be innocent from the great transgression. Let the words of my mouth and the meditation of my heart be acceptable in thy sight O Lord my strength and my redeemer. Psalms 20:1, 2, 6, 7, 8 and 9, The Lord hear thee in the day of trouble the name of the God of Jacob defend thee. Send thee help from the sanctuary and strengthen thee out of Zion. Now know I that the Lord saveth His anointed; He will hear him from His holy heaven with the saving strength of His right hand. Some trust in chariots and some in horses: but we will remember the name of the Lord our God. They are brought down and fallen: but we are risen and stand upright. Save, Lord: Let the King hear us when we call. Psalms 22:27 and 28, All the ends of the world shall remember and turn unto the Lord and all the kindreds of the nations shall worship before thee. For the kingdom is the Lord's and He is the governor among the nations. (24:1) The Earth is the Lord's and the fulness thereof; the world and they that dwell therein. (24:9) Lift up your heads O ye gates; even lift them up ye everlasting doors; the King of glory shall come in. (25:2) O my God, I trust in thee: Let me not be ashamed. Let not mine enemies triumph over me. (24:14) The secret of the Lord is with them that fear Him; and He will show them His covenant. (15) Mine eyes are ever toward the Lord for He shall pluck my feet out of the net. (27:1) The Lord is my light and my salvation; whom shall I fear? The Lord is the strength of my life, of whom shall I be afraid? When the wicked, even mine enemies and my foes came upon me to eat up my flesh, they stumbled and fell. Though an host should encamp against me, my heart shall not fear: though war should rise against me in this will I be confident. (4) One thing have I desired of the Lord that I will seek after; that I may dwell in the house of the Lord all the days of my life to behold the beauty of the Lord and to inquire in His temple. For in the time of trouble He shall hide me in his pavilion: in the secret of His tabernacle shall He hide me; He shall set me upon a rock. And now, shall mine Head be lifted up above mine enemies round about me: therefore will I offer in His tabernacle sacrifices of joy. I will sing, yea I will sing praises unto the Lord. (28:7) The Lord is my strength and my shield; my heart trusted in Him, and I am helped: therefore my heart greatly rejoiceth; and with my song will I praise Him. (8) The Lord is their strength and He is the saving strength of His anointed. (29:11) The Lord will give strength unto His people; the Lord will bless His people with peace. (31:4) Pull me out of the net that they have laid privily for me: for thou art my strength. (5) Into thine hand I commit my spirit: thou hast redeemed me O Lord God of truth. (21) Blessed be the Lord: for He hath shown me His marvelous kindness in a strong city. (32:6) For this shall every one that is godly pray unto thee in a time when thou mayest be found: surely in the floods of great waters they shall not come nigh unto him. (7) Thou art my hiding place thou shalt preserve me from trouble; thou shalt compass me about songs of deliverance. (8) I will instruct thee and teach thee in the way which though shalt go: I will guide thee with mine eye."

These Scriptures became something I read out loud every day. The more I read them, the more I believed in His promises and Him. As my faith grew, the more I believed that the authority I have in Him overpowers the powers of darkness. As I studied more and more of the Bible, I began to see a common prayer when it came to trusting in God to be delivered out of the hands of the enemy. The prayers of David that God showed me are reflected throughout Scripture. Hebrews 4:7 encourages us to pray as David did (saying in David) in faith to enter God's rest. David was a prime example of walking in the power of God to claim victory over the attack. God called David, the least and smallest of his brothers, to face the biggest rivals. Goliath was the first of many. Even as a young shepherd, David was able to kill bears and lions. As he grew older and continued to walk in the steps of the Lord, he faced and conquered impossible odds leading him to win wars for Israel and Judah. David was the ultimate example of being triumphant. God used the least experienced and qualified to prove His glory even further to others. Nothing demonstrates the glory of God more than to use the least likely person to have victory over others. All God requires to use you and me too is a willing and humbled heart. David may have screwed up many times, but there was one thing he had down: trusting and loving God.

God told me awhile back, "If you're still worrying, you're not fully trusting." It's such a simple yet profound reminder to keep myself in check. The moment I start to vocalize my doubts, I stop in my tracks and say that to myself. "If I'm still worrying, I'm not fully trusting." Joshua 10:8 says, "Do not be afraid of them; I have given them into your hand. Not one of them will be able to withstand you." I declare Scriptures over every situation and trust in God to lead me in the next step. He also lets me know when I need to step back and let Him take over. How does He let me know? When I intentionally tune into Him, I get a feeling of peace or discomfort in each situation. The more you tune into Him, the more you will learn to decipher how He communicates to you. It may be a deep gut feeling or a clear telltale sign in some other form. Key is, before each step you take, you have to reach out to Him. When you do, He honors you. He will make way for clear direction, trust me.

I'll give you an example of trying to be in tune with Him. Over a year ago, I was led to write a book. Not this book a different one. It took me nine months to write it, but I managed to finish. I was so proud of it. It was the very first book I had ever written. It was all laid out for the publisher. I had the cover finished and all. However, right around the time I finished it, God started giving me intense dreams. He was communicating Himself to me as He had never done before. I knew it had to be for a reason, so I paused on getting the other book published. I had lost peace to pursue it further at the time. And, nothing seemed to be falling into place to get it published. Anytime I tried to move forward, I would feel held back in some way. The moment I recognized it, I went to God and asked Him to point me in the right direction. I was frustrated in a way because I had worked so hard on it. However, I knew I had to trust Him. Before long, He led me to start this book.

I may not ever get that other one out, or maybe I will. But, for now, I am called to wait. I could have gotten frustrated, but leaning on Him has allowed me to see a different and better perspective. I see now that writing the other book has prepped me to get into a place to write this one. It led me to seek Him further and on a deeper level. The other book took me nine months to write. As of now, this book took me a little over a month. That is how I know it's God. When it's Him, things just fall into place so much easier. I'm not trying to force something to happen. He has taken me so much deeper as I trust Him.

Trust develops as we learn His character. It unfolds as we become one with Him. The Bible tells us that we are the

Body of Christ and that He is the Head. We are part of Him when we accept and believe in Him. For some reason, I had a misconception of the term "body." I use to perceive it as a "body of water" or a "body of people" concept instead of an actual human body. I would see it as a general grouping of people, and He was the leader. I didn't picture it as a connection of a single, unified being. When I took the time to see and define what the Scripture was portraying, the lightbulb went off. Duh! Sometimes I can skim over something so fast; I miss the power it's trying to convey. We are one together, everything He has, we have because it flows from the Head to the Body.

When we accept Jesus, then we have all authority over the darkness that Jesus has. We just have to learn how to utilize that authority. The moment we believe in Jesus is the moment we receive the power we have IN and THROUGH Him. Hebrews 13:6, "So we say with confidence, 'The Lord is my helper; I will not be afraid. What can mere mortals do to me"? Look at Ephesians 6:10—18. It says that we are to put on the "full armor of God" daily; the "belt of truth," the "breastplate of righteousness," the "gospel of peace," the "helmet of salvation," and the "sword of the Spirit." What does all that mean? Well, salvation (believing in Him to save us) will serve as a helmet to protect us when we fall, to protect our thoughts and mind. The belt of truth (God's Word and who He says He is and who we are) holds all of our armor together and strengthens our core. In ancient times, the belt would be the first thing the soldier would put on. His belt held the sword and the rest of his garments in place. It was the foundation underneath his battle gear. The truth is what keeps our "gear" in place when doubt tries to make us question. The breastplate for a soldier was to protect the vital organs of the body, especially the heart.

I believe righteousness is demonstrated as we walk closely with the voice of the Holy Spirit. That's why Noah, Moses, Elijah, and David were referenced in Scripture as being righteous because they walked uprightly in or with the Lord. They talked to Him and understood His intentions and characteristics. They listened to His voice, which kept them protected. His voice leads and directs us, keeping us from harm. It guards our hearts. The sword of the Spirit is the weapon of offense we have over the enemy. It's the Scriptures we declare and proclaim daily. Hebrews 4:12 says,

"The Word of God is alive and active. Sharper than any double-edged sword, it penetrates even to dividing soul and spirit, joints and marrow; it judges the thoughts and attitudes of the heart." The Scriptures are what penetrate and shake up the lies of the enemy. The shoes of the "gospel of peace" are what we walk on. Our feet are grounded in the peace of the Lord. As long as we are confident in the peace that He has given to us, we will continue to stand. We won't allow the lies of Satan to convince us that we are weak. Ephesians 6 says, "Put on the full armor of God so that you can take your stand against the devil's schemes. Our struggle is not against flesh and blood, but against the rulers of the darkness of this world, against the authorities of evil in the heavenly realms. Put on the full armor of God so that when the day of evil comes, you may be able to stand your ground."

Months back, I had come across an evangelist named John Ramirez. The incredible back story of his journey took him from being a Satanist to a born-again Christian. I highly recommend you look him up to hear his testimony. One of the things he said stuck with me, he said as a practicing Satanist, he would meet with the devil face to face. They would meet just like people in a Bible study meet at church. He, and others involved, would devise detailed plans throughout the year to take down Christians and people going against the schemes of Satan. People hired him to conjure up curses on other people. He said the busiest months of the year for practicing Satanists are October and December. It struck a chord in me when he said, "When Christians were out Christmas shopping, trying to decide what size shirt to buy, we would spend all hours of the night devising plans to attack the naive church." I was blown away. I had a hard time believing it honestly. The more I dug into what he said, the more I realized how real it indeed was. He ended up surrendering his life to God when Jesus came to him in a vision after he began to question situations that were taking place. His main lesson to the church today is not to fall into an oblivious mindset of what the devil tries to do. Satan works overtime devising strategies. He dedicates night and day to perfecting his execution. Meanwhile, Christians have a hard time spending five minutes with God. That was a wake-up call for me. It gave me some firm convictions about my relationship with my Lord and Father.

Maybe the reason we are always feeling overwhelmed and beaten down is that we are playing into Satan's hands. We can't win by living in a defensive mode. It will eventually wear us down—life is not about surviving, but about conquering. Becoming stronger requires us to equip ourselves spiritually. We are so busy being oblivious to the spiritual realm. It's like we deny the existence of the things we cannot see. Oxygen is invisible to us, yet we don't deny its existence. Just because we can't see it, doesn't mean it doesn't exist. We can't be so naive.

We can't exercise the authority that Christ promises us if we don't spend time accessing and practicing it. We can't practice the declarations of what the Bible tells us if we don't know what the Bible even says. We have to learn the Word, bottom line. I was living in fear and anxiety before I spent time studying Scripture. You can't expect to face your enemy if you aren't fully equipped, period. Of course, Satan will win if he is spending more time practicing his craft than we are spending time with Jesus. The moment I feel oppressed, I have to stop and look back at how much time I spent studying the Word. How much time did I spend praising and trusting in Jesus? Whatever you give more focus to is what will manifest more powerfully in your life.

Christ died, went beyond the grave, and faced hell to defeat the strongholds that the grave had over us. He made a pathway for us, from death to life in Him, beyond our current natural world. 1 Corinthians 15:55—57, "Death, where is your sting? Grave, where is your victory? Thanks be to God who gives us the victory through our Lord Jesus Christ." Death cannot imprison us. What is typically the biggest fear we have on Earth? We fear death the most right? We hold on so tightly to the things of this world that we are afraid to lose them. However, when we live our life connecting to heaven first, we have such a grander concept beyond what we currently have. We don't view death as a loss, but as a transition of more to gain. That's why Ecclesiastes 7:1 says, "The day of death is better than the day of one's birth." It's because being "kingdom-minded" sees life no matter what. Death does not exist. It's just life leading into greater life.

Through Jesus, the enemy has no stronghold over us. Christ gave us authority and power to bind the princes of darkness (aka principalities). Matthew 16:19, "I will give unto thee the keys of the kingdom of heaven: and whatsoever thou shalt bind on Earth shall be bound in heaven: and whatsoever thou shalt loose on Earth shall be loosed in heaven." Do you realize that people who follow in the ways of Satan loosen these dark forces onto the Earth? Some people may not even be aware of what they are doing and that Satan is guiding them. People conjure and summon up dark spirits. Sometimes they do this thinking they are summoning "good spirits." Anytime you call upon something other than Jesus, it ain't gonna be good my friend. Satan is lying to you, telling you it's some distant relative.

These things happen whether we choose to believe it or deny it. Just as much as the devil can use people to summon, Jesus allows us to possess the power to combat it. We can call on God who surrounds us with angels that fight for and protect us. Through Jesus, we can bind what the enemy has loosened here on Earth. I know this can sound so bizarre and extremely "out there," but demonic activity is very real. I've seen it, and I can never deny it again. I lived in oblivion for way too long, and I unknowingly was imprisoned within the oppression of it. He has shown me what it means to live in victory, and it's only accomplished by leaning on Him. All it takes is us believing we have received what He has already done.

I urge you, spend time with Him. He will teach you how to walk in victory. He will teach you how to allow angels to fight your battles. With each Scripture, you declare out loud, the sword of the Spirit, His Word, penetrates the ways of Satan. Ephesians 2:2 says that Satan is the "prince of the power of the air." That's why we need to speak out loud to him. Satan is not omniscient like God; he doesn't know our thoughts. He only enters in when we allow him. Once our words leave our mouth, they go into the air. They can either be used for him or against him. Always remember that. Speaking into the air manifests the frequencies of the Word of God. It triumphs over the frequencies that are coming against us, which includes harmful frequencies used through technology or ANYTHING that could be potentially harmful to us. God's frequencies are higher than them all! Shout those declarations of victory and praise frequencies into the air, out loud, out of your mouth!

When I say frequencies, I'm talking about the vibrational forces within the air. Every single molecule and particle operate using vibrations and frequencies. Scientists have been researching frequencies for years. There is evidence comparing good vs. bad frequencies. Scientists have proven that they can either be life-giving or harmful. A scientist by the name of Masaru Emoto did an excellent study on this. He compared the effects of negative vs. positive words spoken out loud and how they can affect the environment, including our health. He even measured the frequency vibrations of prayer and noticed it had incredible beneficial effects on the human body. Culture trains us to seek signs to prove God? How can it get more obvious than that?

How can we overcome things that come against us if we can't identify the source of the attack and believe in the authority God tells us we have? Hebrews 2:7-9 says that through Him, He crowns us with glory so that "everything is under them (us who are Christ's). God left nothing that is not subject to them." EVERYTHING is made subject to the power of God. Colossians 2:9, "For in Him the whole fulness of deity dwells bodily." In Him, we obtain His FULL authority. When we believe that we possess that power, we rise above the plans of the enemy. I know I keep referring to the term "enemy," it is anything that is not standing within the ways of God. Matthew 12:30, "He that is not with me is against me." Anything of God is for our benefit. That means anything NOT with God is for our harm. Sometimes the harmful may appear as something beneficial; that's why it is so crucial to train your ear and mind to the promptings and presence of the Holy Spirit.

The world around you may try to convince you that you are weak. That is a lie. If it's not life-giving to you, it is not of God. Don't believe it, and certainly don't identify within it. Identify yourself with who Christ says you are. The way you find out your identity in Him is to study what the Bible says. There's a reason why it stood the test of time. Scriptures are powerful. It helps you recognize the characteristics of Christ and who you are supposed to be in Him. You are strong. You are a warrior of triumph. The moment you start to doubt that, lean on Him. He'll give you the peace and confidence to stand secure. Remember, put on the shoes of the "gospel of peace." YOU ARE MORE THAN A CONQUERER. Satan is a liar, and he knows you are more powerful than him. His lies are the weapon he uses to convince you otherwise. Stay encouraged and stand courageous because, through Christ, all things are possible to those who believe.

Psalms 56:4—11, "In God I will praise His word, in God I have put my trust; I will not fear what flesh can do unto me. Every day they wrest my words: all their thoughts are against me for evil. When I cry unto thee, then shall mine enemies turn back: this I know; for God is for me. In God have I put my trust: I will not be afraid what man can do unto me."

• CHAPTER 9 •

Redemption

Redemption has possibly become one of the most underrated concepts in the Christian faith. I believe many have overlooked the power of His redemptive love and mercy. I say this because I did myself. A big lesson I've learned this year, NEVER limit God. NEVER put God in a box, ESPECIALLY when it comes to His love, His redemption, and the supernatural power of the glory of His grace.

What is redemption? In the Bible, it is the atonement for sin for those who are separated from God. As we look deeper into its definition, redemption is a ransom or price paid in full that redeemed humanity, reconciling us back to God.

We receive redemption by faith in Jesus Christ as we repent, accept, and believe that through His death on the Cross, we have been ransomed or rescued from the kingdom of darkness and brought into His kingdom of light.

According to Isaiah 59:1, "The Lord's hand is not shortened, that it cannot save: neither His ear heavy, that it cannot hear." Approaching God isn't complicated. Don't let the lies convince you that's it's some qualifying race to make you worthy enough to receive God's glory and redemption. All it takes is faith in Jesus Christ and to love Him and others wholeheartedly. Jesus answers a man in Luke 10:25—28 when He was inquiring about what will give him access to eternal life. Jesus had him repeat what was written in the "law." The man stated, "Love the Lord your God with all your heart and with all your soul and with all your strength and with all your mind and, love your neighbor as yourself." Jesus said, "Thou has answered right." That's it. Loving Jesus wholeheartedly is why we received a rebirth, and it is the foundation for restoration in Him. All of our works and good deeds follow the reality of our hearts. The works are the outworking of a willing or unwilling heart, not the cause of the willing heart. Ephesians 2:8-9, "For by grace are ye saved through faith; and that not of yourselves: it is the gift of God: Not of works, lest any man should boast." If we define our pass into heaven by the things we do, all of us will fall short. That's why the Lord so favored David. David understood he was no more significant than the person next to him. He considered himself a sinner like the rest. He lovingly saw people just as the Father did. He wanted to bring life to others, not oppression. We may not agree with the things that people do. They may be doing things that aren't pleasing to God. However, God alone knows the heart. He knows when the heart is genuine, submissive, humbled, and willing to love. He doesn't need help judging the heart.

I don't agree with many actions that people do. Sometimes it does make me sick to my stomach. Yes, many times, people are in the wrong. The thing is, I'm still called to bring them life and to show the love of Jesus. If I'm constantly looking at people through a lens that only recognizes their sins or faults, it puts a spirit of oppression and shame over them and me. It makes people feel less worthy to receive the Father. Let me tell you something, we ALL fall short of the glory of God. Not one person on the planet is deserving of His goodness, yet He chooses to freely give it to us.

2 Peter 3:9 says, "The Lord is not slack concerning His prom-ise, as some men count slackness; but is long-suffering to us-ward, not willing that any should perish, but that all should come to repentance."

Jesus is a life-giver. One of the main reasons why people are leaving the church and turning away from God is because they aren't experiencing an in-depth Holy Spirit encounter and relationship with Christ. Quite honestly, I don't believe it's being modeled enough through others. The Bible says that in order for us to know God, the Holy Spirit within us teaches us, not man alone, but the Holy Spirit (1John 2:27. Jesus left us a Helper, who He said would also comfort us. The Holy Spirit, who is also according to Jesus, the Spirit of Truth, who will lead and guide us into all truth. Believers should be leading by example through the guidance of the Holy Spirit. If you spend time with Him, you will take on His characteristics, become like Him, and that will draw people to want to know Him on their own. Some people might feel shame because of the church's unrighteous judgment. I know it may not always be the intention of the church to bring shame, but it's what happens when people aren't fully walking with or being led by the Holy Spirit.

When we walk in the characteristics of the Father, we exude His goodness to others. Romans 2:4 says, "the goodness of God leadeth thee to repentance." People will be drawn to God when they recognize the goodness we pour into their lives. The church needs to be so conscientious of bringing life to people through words and actions. Remember, how we judge and behave toward others is how we will be judged. 1 Peter 4:17-19 says, "For the time is come that judgment must begin at the house of God: and if it first begin at us, what shall the end be of them that obey not the Gospel of God? And if the righteous scarcely be saved, where shall the ungodly and the sinner appear? Wherefore let them that suffer according to the will of God commit the keeping of their souls to him in well doing, as unto a faithful Creator."

I believe so many people have misinterpreted this Scripture. It's mainly because the original meaning got lost in different translations of the text. This Scripture is a prime example of how important it is to pull up the original language text. Greek was the language of The New Testament. Most English versions interpret verse 19 as saying, "commit the keeping of their souls" is referring to the keeping of their souls. Some versions even say, "those who suffer according to God's will should commit themselves to their faithful Creator and continue to do good."

We have to be so careful with all these different translations. I like to read from the King James version because it's pretty close to the original transfer over to English. I still like to pull up the original language, though. When you pull up the original text for this verse, it reads "*paratithesthosan tas psychos auton.*" It directly translates into "let them commit the souls of them." In other Bible references where those exact words appear, they also describe taking care of those around you. The Holy Spirit spoke to me when reading this and said, "The church is not to ignore the disobedient and rebellious ones like some of the translations would elude, they are to take care of the keeping of their souls." That's the whole point of including the ungodly reference within those verses. We are to love their souls. We are to continue to pray for the pressing of the Holy Spirit on their hearts. We are to go to spiritual battle for their salvation.

The Holy Spirit teaches us what is right and wrong in the eyes of the Father. He also trains us on how to see through

God's lens that always loves and desires to save people. People often argue what's right or wrong with someone, but they do it unknowingly operating under selfish intentions. It stems out of a desire to be correct, instead of out of a motive to save a soul. I have done this myself. It's so easy for anyone to fall into this behavior. We have to keep ourselves in check when it comes to recognizing sin and proving the truth of the Father. Ask yourself, "Am I doing this to prove a point and win an argument, or am I doing it to care for someone and save their soul"? People can sense whether or not you're in it to bring them life, or to bring them shame and death. If you feel yourself getting frustrated, pause, and take a step back. We must be careful to not be led by our emotions when we respond to others. Seek the Holy Spirit and what God says about the matter. Scriptures always speak the truth even when you don't know how. Talk about the Father's goodness and the life He brings when we walk with Him. If things start to heat up, stop and ask, "Is this life-giving"?

Ezekiel 13:22 says that the hands of the wicked "promise life." We know that's how Satan lures people in. He's a deceiver. We have to be so careful as lovers of Christ not to bring focus on what will happen to disobedient people, but on what will happen to them when they turn to Christ. Remember, people who aren't fully walking in the security of Christ will be affected more by the deception of Satan. He will make them focus on the negative rather than the life-giving positive. When you're walking close with God, He makes you feel so valued and loved. He makes me want to pour all of His love out on others. If more people were drawn to the life and love of Christ, instead of bringing focus to where they fall short of it, more souls would be won to Jesus. Our focus should be zoomed in on the goodness of God and tuned to the Holy Spirit's voice.

People who don't believe in God or Christ always have similar reasons as to why. So many people say, "I can't believe in a God who sends people to hell for eternity." I used to struggle with this one too. I would question, "If God is such a loving Father, how does this happen"? It's okay to ask, that's when trust and faith kick in. If you trust that He's in it for your good, turn to Him to find the reasons why Scriptures say the things that they say. Sometimes, it's because we don't comprehend His eternal intentions. Sometimes it may not be the right time for Him to reveal them entirely either.

It wasn't until recently that God started showing me a more profound concept of His redemption. He always wants to bring forth life and gives opportunity after opportunity to us to choose life with Him. I've discovered how loving, powerful, and purposeful God is. I genuinely believe that in an appointed time, Scriptures say in "due time," His wondrous glory will manifest upon the people who seek Him. They will exude His redeeming love, making Christ evident to those who they are praying for to receive salvation. The people who pray are called in the Bible, intercessors. They cry out to Jesus in times of need, knowing that He is the Author and Finisher of their faith. He is the righteous Savior. Romans 8:27, "And He that searcheth the hearts knoweth what is the mind of the Spirit because He maketh intercession for the saints according to the will of God."

God appointed us from the womb to be saved and to experience eternal life with Him in heaven. I believe that the Lamb's book of Life has the names of everyone who is formed in the womb. Psalms 139:16, "Thine eyes did see my substance, yet being unperfect; and in thy book all my members were written, which in continuance were fashioned, when as yet there was none of them." He appointed us to live with Him from the beginning. What was written in the beginning is what stands firm throughout eternity. Revelation 3:5, "He who overcomes will thus be clothed in white garments; and I will not erase his name from the book of life, and I will confess his name before My Father and before His angels." Jesus only blots it out when you refuse Him. If people decide to continue in their rejection of the Father, then they choose death. But God wants you to enter in. He doesn't want to blot your name out. It's the devil who blinds us. The devil is trying to hold us hostage so we cannot see the truth about Christ; all we see is ourselves.

We were created to worship God and come to know Him, which is why I think Scripture says the devil is sitting there waiting for the birth to devour (Revelation 12:4). He was looking to destroy Jesus from birth, and he's looking to destroy and devour us, the seed of Jesus. He's trying to steal from God's appointed Book of Life that was written from the foundations of the world. It is God's will and heart for us who were formed in the womb to have life with Him. The devil and his demonic spirits (fallen angels) are doing everything they can to destroy the plans of God. They bring temptation to man and create the stumbling blocks of the flesh. Don't let Satan lie to you and think that because God knows all that He's the one responsible for sending people to hell. He has appointed us to be with Him in heaven. We are the ones who choose not to be. He always leaves us with the freedom to choose Him. When we seek Him, we will find Him. The more we seek Him, the more we get to know Him. As our relationship grows together, we see through His lens of hope and life.

Regarding free will, it's God's love that allows us to freely choose Him. He's done everything within His power to provide an abundant life for us. Jesus destroyed the power of Satan on the Cross. When we choose to believe in Christ, we discover the Father's eternal intentions.

As you learn and grow with Him, He will point you to Scriptures to give you hope and understanding so you will have peace and be able to comfort others in that hope. If you utilize and walk-in full spiritual authority like discussed in the previous chapter, He will give you the power to break strongholds in your life. He will give you keys to unlock chains in other people's lives when they come to you for help. Once their eyes are opened, and the lies of the enemy are destroyed, their stumbling blocks are removed. In Matthew 19:24, Jesus told His disciples it is easier for a camel to go through the eye of a needle than for a rich man to enter the Kingdom of God. Here's their response, "When His disciples heard it, they were exceedingly amazed, saying, Who then can be saved? But Jesus beheld them, and said unto them, with men, this is impossible; but with God, all things are possible" (v. 25 & 26). Jesus can turn even the hardest of hearts. Romans 5:6 says, "In due time, Christ died for the ungodly." Isaiah 42:16, "I will make darkness light before them, and crooked things straight. These things will I do unto them, and not forsake them."

You might be remembering Scriptures like Matthew 7:23, "Then will I profess unto them, I never knew you: depart from me, ye that work iniquity." The lies of Satan will make you look at this Scripture and only see the separation part of it. Satan makes Jesus appear to you like it was His intention from the beginning to cast people away from Him. I was confused by this too. He'll make you think, "If Scripture also says He comes to save the lost, then why does He separate Himself from them"? It seems like a reasonable question, right?

As I began learning the characteristics of the Father, He led me to read further into the intention behind the separation. He says this to people who choose to still harden their hearts toward life with Him. It's not that He wants to forsake. He never got to know them because they didn't allow Him to. It wasn't necessarily Him rejecting, it was the choice of the people who forsook Him. I do feel; however, it is possible for Him to show mercy even beyond the moment He declares they are forsaken. He gives opportunities over and over for people to choose Him just as He did with Ephraim.

In Jeremiah 7:15, God says that He cast out Ephraim and the entire seed. However, in Hosea Chapters 11 through 14, God talks about coming again to heal them. Hosea 11:9 and 10, "I will not execute the fierceness of mine anger, I will not return to destroy Ephraim: for I am God, and not man; the Holy One in the midst of thee... They shall walk after the Lord." God is always looking to save, even in the last hour. When people humble their pride and repent of their mistakes, He sees their softened heart. He's longing for people to accept His goodness. Then I read Isaiah 54:7—10, "For a small moment have I forsaken thee; but with great mercies will I gather thee. In a little wrath I hid my face from thee for a moment; but with everlasting kindness will I have mercy on thee, saith the Lord thy Redeemer. For this is as the waters of Noah unto me: for as I have sworn that the waters of Noah should no more go over the Earth; so have I sworn that I would not be wroth with thee, nor rebuke thee. For the mountains shall depart, and the hills be removed; but my kindness shall not depart from thee, neither shall the covenant of my peace be removed, saith the Lord that hath mercy on thee." We were all once forsaken sinners, but Jesus was sent to be our redemption. And, I believe that the message of the Gospel will continue to turn hearts toward Jesus up to the final Judgement Day before the destruction of the Earth. Who's to say it won't? God is always trying to find a way to save. I believe that this could be a possibility. I'll explain why in a second.

What Jesus did on the Cross was proof that He wanted to make a way for us to be with Him in heaven for eternity. He gave up His life to conquer the stronghold of death, hell, and the grave. If He were not our once for all sacrifice, our sins would keep us unclean to enter into a state of perfection in heaven. Jesus' blood continually cleanses us and makes us whole so that we are ready to be made perfect and washed in Him in order to enter. If corruption entered heaven, then it would be just how it is here on Earth currently. God wants to completely get rid of suffering for His children. Heaven wouldn't be considered paradise with sin and suffering. He even gives us a way to escape torment here on Earth until we enter heaven. He's such a good Father, always trying to comfort His children. When Jesus died on the Cross, our sins and our torment were nailed there, and the lies of Satan destroyed if we choose to believe in Christ and utilize the authority, we have in Him.

I believe the above Scripture from Isaiah ties into Matthew 24:37, "But as the days of Noah were, so shall also the coming of the Son of man be." So many of us focus on what happened to the people in flood. We see the death and separation that occurred and think that's what it was referencing. We don't acknowledge that it was their choice not to be saved. He didn't force His saving grace on them.

Satan makes us feel that Jesus is coming to judge and destroy. Jesus came to save the lost. His redeeming love is inside of those who choose Him, and when we express His love, it overflows onto others. He's called us to comfort them so they can believe in Him too. He's trying to press on us to do our part to make way for others. Some days I feel like, He's crying out, begging us to bring others away from destruction.

I believe that yes, there WILL be a separation of the elect and those who refuse Jesus before the Great Day of the Lord, which is described throughout Scripture as the Second Coming of Jesus Christ and the Final Judgment. However, according to my hope and what I think Scriptures seem to reflect in Revelation, God still gives many opportunities for salvation during the Tribulation period to those left behind after the Rapture before they have to face the final judgment and everlasting fire. Through the Gospel and you and me, He's pleading with people to wake up so they won't face that. 2 Corinthians 5:20 says, "Now then we are ambassadors for Christ, as though God did beseech you by us: we pray you in Christ's stead, be ye reconciled to God."

The devil tries to convince you that Jesus is the one who appoints you to death. Not true! Why would God create you to destroy you? That is not His will. He's only looking to comfort you. Here's the thing, I would do anything I could to save my kid. However, if they willingly refuse to heed my warnings that keep them safe and choose to jump in a fire when I tell them it will destroy them, they have that choice. I will put up a fight, I will be willing to give up my life, but if they push me away and do it anyway, that was their decision. It would break my heart, but they had to make their own choice. God is the same with His children (you are a child of God) He didn't create robots. That's not a way to true love.

I think that the separation of the elect is also used to help intercede in the healing and comforting of those when He comes back the second time just before the final judgment. I believe the elect are the intercessors with Jesus, and that they will come back to search for life, just like the doves did out of the windows of the ark. The windows of the ark, I think, symbolized the windows of heaven. Isaiah 60:8 says, "Who are these that fly as a cloud, and as the doves to their windows." Jesus comes the second time, surrounded by a cloud. I believe this is why Revelation says that He will appear with a bow (rainbow) on His head when He returns. That, to me, is symbolic of the sign of His promise to Noah never to judge the Earth by flood as He did before. When He judged the wicked before, He shut the door to them who didn't believe the warnings of Noah. I believe that the Holy Spirit is showing me that Jesus is our continual intercessor in the time of appointed death that they are choosing to put over themselves, to give another chance to redeem and heal souls.

2 Thessalonians 2:8 says, "And then shall that Wicked be revealed, who the Lord shall consume with the spirit of his mouth, and shall destroy with the brightness of His coming." Get that? Just the mere brightness of God's glory will destroy the Wicked one. There is no battle. There won't have to be. That Second Coming of Jesus from the song of the saints trailing with Him, will remove the veil from those left.

If they choose to continue in their rebellion to God, then that's their choice. The thing is, when I'm a part of those intercessors with Jesus, when I'm a part of that great army, I will do whatever I can to save the lost and show them the life I found in Jesus. Ya'll, take my word for it, there is no greater hope. There is no greater love. Don't let Satan tell you God's in it to appoint people to death.

2 Corinthians 3:16-17, "When it shall turn to the Lord, the veil shall be taken away. Now the Lord is that Spirit: and

where the Spirit of the Lord is, there is freedom." On that great day of His Second Coming, after the Tribulation, I hope people will choose the One who remains victorious. I think that's also why Scripture calls it the "Great and Terrible Day of the Lord." You have the power to choose either. All of us will be victorious when we open our eyes and receive Christ as Savior. At least that's my hope and what I will choose to believe. Matthew 21:22, "And all things, whatsoever ye shall ask in prayer, believing, ye shall receive." That's what I will choose to walk in from this day to that last day. As long as I live, I will comfort and love those to help them find salvation through faith in Jesus so that they can see His hope and goodness from now to the end of the Earth as we know it.

When you experience His glory, His full glory, He is so great that all you want to do is bow down and worship Him. I feel that's how the Great Day of His Second Coming will look like as well. He's here right now trying to save. And, I believe He's coming again to save even within His wrath of justice. Yes, there will be great destruction and turmoil in the seven years of Tribulation. However, it's for those who refuse Jesus and repentance to worship Satan. This is why

I believe Scriptures in Revelation say a "third of the Earth" during the plagues in the Tribulation. Satan brings that over the heads of those who worship him. That's why it is so important to be tuned into the voice of the Holy Spirit in those days to avoid confusion. For those who understand the power they have through Jesus and the Holy Spirit, they know they have authority over whatever comes against them. In Revelation Chapter 13, the Scriptures talk about the power given to the beast to overcome the saints. However, God is still in control. That's why I believe verses 9 and 10 say, "If ANY man have an ear let him ear." "He that leadeth into captivity will go into captivity, and he that killeth with the sword must be killed with the sword." To me, the "he" is ANYONE that is utilizing the authority they have in Christ Jesus. I believe this is there to tell us that whoever is obeying the promises of His Word and following His Spirit, you will have the ability to triumph, even when it appears impossible. "Killing with the sword" to me means that His saints are speaking His Word over the powers of darkness. He has given us victory, and God is always in control, even in the face of the Antichrist. Walking in the redemption and promises of God also gives us peace and victory through the Tribulation. He has given His saints patience and perseverance through ALL tribulation, which to me INCLUDES the Great Tribulation as well. Matthew 28:20, "I am with you always, even unto the end of the world."

Mercy is always found in the wrath of destruction. Isaiah 54:8, "In a little wrath I hid my face from thee for a moment; but with everlasting kindness will I have mercy on thee, saith the LORD thy Redeemer." God hid His face from Jesus for a moment on The Cross so Christ could pay the full price for sin, sickness, and death. It must have pained Him to do it, but it was necessary. Just like with us, it's not that He wants to hide his face. When we don't choose Him and choose His protection from the enemy's pathway to destruction, we're the ones that hide our face from Him. Evil cannot be in His presence it must be destroyed, restoration must come, so all rebellion and sin will be removed to establish His Kingdom on Earth. He doesn't want us to be a part of that destruction. That's why He gets angry when we choose it, just like we get mad at our kids for being rebellious. He's so frustrated with the fact that we can't see to get out of the way of destruction. When we choose to get out of the way after humbling ourselves and admitting He

IS the one Who's appointed life, then we are immediately set free from the destruction that tries to rule us.

An example of this is what God did with the people in Nineveh. In Jonah 3:9 and 10, "Who can tell if God will turn and repent, and turn away from His fierce anger, that we perish not? When God saw their works, that they turned from their evil way, then God repented concerning the calamity which He had declared He would bring upon them. And He did not do it." Yes, in the deception of the Wicked one, people are appointed to destruction because he's trying to steal them from God and bring them with him. However, God can choose to forgive them, and redeem and heal them when they repent and make Christ their Lord. Psalms 102:20, "To hear the groaning of the prisoner; to loose those that are appointed to death." John 5:21-22 says, "For as the Father raiseth up the dead, and quickeneth them; even so the Son quickeneth whom He will. For the Father judgeth no man, but hath committed all judgment unto the Son." Jesus' vengeance took place on the Cross. His vengeance was to redeem those who even go against Him. He made a way for them to receive life through Him when they choose Him.

He became sin to defeat it. Don't let the blinders of sin make you think He's not in it for your good.

Jesus gave us the power to be intercessors for those who are blinded by the plan of the enemy. Satan is trying to take them out of the Book of Life. I'm sorry, but I REFUSE to let him have anyone around me. So, I encourage you to fight for those around you through prayer. Don't accept the devil appointing them to death. We have to become so passionate to preach the Gospel of the love and redemption of Christ. Romans 1:16 says the Gospel of Christ is "the power of God unto salvation to everyone that believeth." The power of Christ is in you and has given you the ability to be the doorway of salvation for others to see Jesus and salvation through Him. So, you can show them that they have power over the Tribulation and are not appointed to suffer. People are not meant for it. You don't have to shove yourself in their face about it, but show them the goodness, the kindness, and the love of Jesus. Point them to the way of life.

Psalms 8:6, "Thou madest him to have dominion over the works of thy hands; thou has put all things under his feet."

They are called to pay attention to His glory when you show them God's glory. His glory is in you when you recognize it and choose to be a demonstration of it. Isaiah 60:3 says that "the place of my feet will be made glorious." Jesus is living in us by way of the Holy Spirit; we just need to release Him through our daily living, words, and deed. We can make the Earth glorious if we will talk with Him in the here and now. In Isaiah 60:6, He says so, "He can bring recompense to his enemies." Then in verse 9, "Shall I bring to the birth and not cause to bring forth? Saith the Lord: shall I cause to bring forth, and shut the womb? Saith thy God." He's calling us to break the chains the enemy has over people. The kingdom of heaven is at hand and literally in us through the power of His presence. His kingdom is HERE!

God's purpose wasn't to shut people out of His kingdom. Psalms 146:9 says, "The Lord preserveth the strangers; He relieveth the fatherless and widow: but the way of the wicked He turned upside down." We have the power to turn the ways of the wicked right now and going forward. God has appointed ministers who will preach the Gospel during the Tribulation and to the last day before the Great Day of the Lord. God is a God of second chances, and we are a part of His second chance offers as we share Christ with everyone around us. People have to wake up and take it. 2 Peter 3:9, "The Lord is not slow to fulfill His promise as some count slowness, but is patient toward you, not wishing that any should perish, but that all should reach repentance."

Jesus came to fulfill the will of the Father. Luke 5:32, "I have not come to call the righteous, but sinners to repentance." Why should we limit the redemption and glory of God? We must stop making heaven a qualifying competition to get in by trying to judge whether or not someone is doing something that prevents them from eternal life. Remember, we are not saved by works, but by grace. We have to fight for others around us. We are called to be intercessors for them.

The world was evil in the days of Noah, but because of Noah's faithfulness, God extended favor to restore. He found favor in Abraham because He was willing to give up His son Isaac which provided a blessing over the rest of His seed that their sins would be recompensed and replaced with the benefits of God if they choose to follow Him (Genesis 22:17). Moses begged God for mercy in Numbers

11:14—16 and was even willing to give up his own life for the sake of others, and God reserved and appointed the righteous Levites to help make way for all. They became the gates to lead the Israelites into the Promise Land. David was willing to lay his life down for God to spare Saul's life, and God promised to save Saul's seed because of it. Stephen cried out to forgive his murderers before he was stoned. Why do I give all these examples? Because those who were willing to love so much that they would give their life for another, is when the greatest love was made known: God's REDEEMING love and mercy. That's why I think Jesus became the permanent example for the rest of us. He possesses the keys to the gates, even to His enemies (Genesis 22:17). He became the ultimate intercessor to open the gate of heaven, and I believe even in the last Great Day of the Lord.

I believe that by faith, there is hope for those up UNTIL the day of Jesus' Second Coming after Tribulation. As spoken by the prophet Joel in Joel 2:11—13, he says, "for the day of the Lord is great and very terrible; and who can endure it"? He later says in verse 13, "Rend your heart, and not your garments, and turn unto the Lord your God: for He is gracious and merciful, slow to anger, and of great kindness, and repenteth Him of the evil," which is also why he says right after to blow the trumpet and gather the people. I believe this is a reference to the 7th trumpet in Revelation and the "song of the 144,000" in Revelation 14:3. I will get into more detail in the next chapters. I believe God was showing me that song was the song of both David and Moses crying out for the redemption of the people. To turn evil to good. To show the goodness of the Father to the others that are about to get caught up in the destruction of the evil. Just like David repaid Saul with life. Again, it references back to the Scripture in Romans, "the goodness of God calls forth repentance." I believe that the elected intercessors with Jesus will be rejoicing and singing praises of victory and goodness and mercy, calling forth repentance of those who choose it. That, to me, also goes hand-in-hand with God's justice for His people. I also believe that's what Revelation 18:4 could be referring to as well when it says, "Come out of her, my people that ye be not partakers of her sins, and that ye receive not of her plagues." To me, this is God calling out, through His intercessors' song, to pull people out to be saved before complete destruction.

Now saying that I'm not saying it gives permission to continue in sin. Hebrews 10:26 says, "For if we sin willfully after that we have received the knowledge of the truth, there remaineth no more sacrifice for sins." Because in that mindset, we won't repent and humble ourselves. We're not allowing Him to make us clean so we can be saved by humility through our repentance and acceptance of Jesus. Also, if we live in sin on Earth, we are harmed and tormented on Earth. Why would we choose that? Why would I take advantage of the One Who has the power of eternity in His hands? I wouldn't dare. Like I said, He judges based on the matters of the heart. I believe He will give a second, a third, a fourth, a fifth chance (as many as time allows), but if people choose to be blind after separation through the Rapture, the longer they are blinded, the more destruction they will feel and face. And all because Satan is deceiving them into believing that it is meant for them.

IF by SOME reason He's calling intercessors to go through the Tribulation, then there is no reason to fear it, because the suffering of the Tribulation is not meant for us. My belief in Him shows me that truth. Hebrews 11:34 says that faith will "quench the violence of fire." He is my hope and my strength, and I will escape destruction whether He will pull me out of it or shows me that I have power over it. I'm going to do what I can to show others that too, which is why I also think the stories of Jesus' healing on the Sabbath were important. The Pharisees called Him a false prophet because He healed the demon-possessed on God's holy seventh day when God rested from His works. I believe that's also why Scripture says that we are not saved by works, but by grace. Healing the demon-possessed flesh on God's holy day is an example of His will to save. It's not about what we do. I believe that His full reappearance on Earth again is considered God's Holy Day because that is the day that He will get rid of all the evil and restore and make everything new. Anytime God makes something new it is considered a Holy day unto Him. I believe that Jesus can heal that last Holy Day right before the appointed death of eternal damnation. I also think that's what Isaiah 62:7 meant when it says, "And give him no rest, till He establishes, and till He makes Jerusalem a praise in the Earth." We are called to see His plan through to the new heavens and Earth. If we choose to see Him as the life-giver that He is, we know that His return will bring forth new life.

Isaiah 42:22 & 23, 43:1, and 8 & 9, "They are all of them snared in holes, and they are hid in prison houses: they are for a prey, and none delivereth; for a spoil, and none saith, Restore. Who among you will give ear to this? Who will hearken and hear the for time to come? Fear not: for I have redeemed thee, I have called thee by thy name; thou art mine. Bring forth the blind people that have eyes, and the deaf that have ears. Let all the nations be gathered together, and let the people be assembled: who among them can declare this, and show us former things? Let them bring forth their witnesses, that they may be justified: or let them hear, and say, It is truth." Jesus is the Way, the Truth, and the LIFE. No man cometh unto the Father except through Him.

God's Word and character always reflect the power of His supernatural grace from the beginning till the end. He will forgive without limit. I urge you to dive deeper into your study of the Word. Don't just take my word for it. Get to know the Father and His character. As I said, no one can teach you that. You must seek Him yourself. He is such a loving Father willing to adopt even strangers into His family. He calls us to love Him and to love others as we would want to be loved. When I'm with Him as an intercessor on that great day, then I will shout in praise to declare His victory tearing down the veil of deception that's blinding those from being saved. I'm living that way from now on. Jesus is my example. He did it for me; He can do it for them too.

• CHAPTER 10 •

The Power of Praise

Praise is one of the most powerful weapons in the spirit realm. It's also the key that unlocks the gates leading us from the natural to the courts of heaven. Psalms 100:4, "Enter His gates with thanksgiving and His courts with praise." God has taught me how to tap into the things He wants to show and give me through praise. The first step is to bust through the walls of distraction that the enemy places in front of you by humbling your heart, letting go of selfish expectations, and bring yourself before Him to get to know His goodness. Entering His holy place calls for true humility. The opposing force of humility is pride, which is the thing that separates us the most from seeing into the heavenly realm. Once we let go of ourselves and our expectations, we can take our first steps into His courtroom. If we want to feel the deepness and the fullness of His presence, His courtroom is where it's at for sure.

Thanksgiving is the first step on the pathway, and it's not just about appreciation for something given like we know it to be. It goes beyond that. Even an arrogant king can thank a pauper for a gift that he considers himself worthy to receive. True thanksgiving is born out of a realization that you're not worthy; however, you're stepping in faith to believe in the One Who is. We don't put faith in our faith; we have faith in Jesus. The Hebrew word for thanksgiving used in this particular Scripture is "*todah*," which comes from the original word "*yadah*." It means to confess by faith. It is an act and expression of stepping in the belief that God is willing and capable of doing all things. We might not have the capability, but trusting that there is One Who does will allow us to have access to that power.

The act of thanksgiving is, in essence, acknowledging that He will take care of you even before you know you need Him to in the natural. It's the expression of admiration toward the Giver Who's considering you valuable enough to receive even when you're not deserving. Thanksgiving flows from a humbled heart of reverence, which allows you to see His magnificent greatness.

The next step to enter His courts after the act of thanksgiving is PRAISE. The Hebrew word for praise in Psalms 100:4 is *"tehhillaw,"* which comes from the root *"halal."* It means to boast. Usually, when you boast, it means that you're bragging about something that has already been done. You've seen and felt the accomplishment, and you're proud and joyful about the result. That's how it is when we praise God. 1 Peter 1:8 & 9 says, "Though you have not seen Him, you love Him. Though you do not now see Him, you believe in Him and rejoice with joy that is inexpressible and filled with glory, obtaining the outcome of your faith, the salvation of your souls." Our faith to trust that He is capable matures us into actually believing that whatever we ask for, according to His will, is achieved. Our belief leads to the joy and acceptance of what He has done. That's how we receive Him. How can we receive Him if we don't fully believe in what He has done and will do? We only obtain to the degree that we believe.

That's when genuine praise is established. That's why strongholds of the enemy shatter in the presence of God, which opens through our praise. It's because praise is an utterance and confession of joy for Him and what He's done! Psalms 106:2, "Who can utter the mighty acts of the Lord? Who can show forth all his praise?" It's the ultimate expression and maturity of our faith. The enemy cannot stand against that kind of faith and praise.

So often, we underestimate and don't fully comprehend the concept of "the power of praise." It's because we aren't choosing to see the things taking place within the spiritual realm. John 4:24 says, "God is a Spirit: and they that worship Him must worship Him in spirit and in truth." What does that mean? I believe it means that we are to be directed and guided by the Spirit first. We operate beyond what is taking place around us and what our physical eyes see. We have to practice tapping into the kingdom. If we believe that the kingdom of heaven is full of glory, power, and victory, we must learn how to reflect that here on Earth. That is God's will for us. Remember, "on Earth as it is in heaven."

God's power is the same here on Earth as it is in heaven. Why do we have such a hard time accepting that on Earth? If we say we believe that He is more powerful than the things that we face, then why do we still walk in doubt? We have to start practicing how to see heaven here on Earth. Psalms 113:6, "Who humbleth himself to behold the things that are in heaven and in the Earth." We must remove our skewed, doubting human perspective, and tap into the goodness of the kingdom of heaven. That's what it means to praise Him in spirit. You're operating in the spiritual realm and allowing it to take place in the natural. You're either the blocker or the receiver, which allows that to happen. Don't let Satan lie to you by saying that it's not possible to have all heavenly power here on Earth. When you fully realize that all power of heaven can be manifested in your life, you're going to be praising so hard and strong that you might quite literally move mountains.

God has been showing me a lot recently that praise is what will cause His enemies to humble and turn. He has given us the ability to turn nations with our faith. Not calling destruction and vengeance on them, but salvation. Combat your doubt and fear with praise. Nothing builds your faith more than praising and boasting in what the Redeemer can do. Praising and declaring salvation for your enemies is the ultimate expression of your faith. David expressed his strong belief in the power of the Father through his praise. He understood the power of praise so much that he vowed to do it all his days (Psalms 145:1 and 2). He believed that through the declaration of praise, all would come to know the power of the One true King. Psalms 145:11 and 12, "They shall speak of the glory of thy kingdom, and talk of thy power; to make known to the sons of men His mighty acts, and the glorious majesty of His kingdom." Then later in verse 21, "My mouth shall speak the praise of the Lord: and let all flesh bless His Holy name for ever and ever." I believe that the glory of Jesus is so powerful that it can make even the utterance of our praise be used to direct souls to salvation through Him. When you declare the goodness of the Father over all, why wouldn't people feel that sense of being drawn to Him? Saving souls for eternal life in the presence of His goodness is the ultimate and absolute will of the Father. Jesus is the Author and Finisher of our faith. If He instills in us a hope of things to come according to His will, shouting praise and thanksgiving in a declaration is what will call it forth. If you want to win souls for Jesus, shout it out in praise. Show them the joy and salvation you have in Jesus.

By faith, you can quench the violence of fire (Hebrews 11:34) over people's lives. God has not appointed them for destruction. Remember how I said one of the first things He told me was to "rise up the Levites"? Well, one of the most important jobs of the Levites was to stand in the gates of the Temple to offer praise before God to allow His favor to move through the kingdom of Israel during the reign of King David. 1 Chronicles 16:4 & 8, "And He appointed certain Levites to minister before the ark of the Lord, and to record, and to thank and praise the Lord God of Israel. Give thanks unto the Lord, call upon His name, make known His deeds among the people." Any sacrifice that the Levites offered up to God was made holy before Him (Numbers 18:9-10). Even the daughters of the Levites took part in this sacrifice. Where all my *sistahs* at these days!?!

When the Levites testified and confessed of the glory and greatness of God, their faith motivated God to move. The Israelites, in their rebellion, saw His marvelous works and surrendered to accept His atonement (what we know today as redemption). The act of faith by the few, caused the multitude to receive God's goodness. Acts 2:47, "Praising God, and having favor with all the people. And the Lord added to the church daily such as should be saved." It starts with a few who understand the power of praise and how to reflect the kingdom of heaven on Earth. His glory comes to touch those around them and soon becomes the rippling effect of saving souls. How powerful is that!?!

Praise was also the method God instructed Joshua to use when facing the walls of Jericho. Jericho was the one thing that was separating the Israelites from crossing over into the land that God promised them. I believe that Jericho was symbolic of what happens in the Spirit. The enemy puts a wall blocking us to receive deliverance and the promises of God. His instructions to march around for seven days giving and shouting praise was used as an instruction manual for us on how to experience breakthrough victory. They first humbled themselves to be obedient to the instructions of God. They trusted and walked by faith, believing that He would deliver. Step 1: thanksgiving. Step 2: praise, the ultimate boasting in what the Lord will do. They were literally walking in the belief that God would deliver. They were praising Him because they saw the walls fall before they did by using their kingdom lens. Their faith that God would move made it happen in the natural. God moved, and Jericho, the kingdom of the enemy, was handed over through their sacrifice of praise. I say sacrifice because their pride and doubt were laid down and sacrificed to shout with praise.

David also perfected the art of praise, he was one of the mightiest men in battle. And, there was a reason God chose a psalmist, musician, and singer who wrote much of the book of Psalms. His writings are like a recipe book on how to draw near to God and defeat enemies. The majority of them were written in song form. You can tell because anytime you see the word "Selah" at the end of a sentence in Psalms, it means that he was pausing to reflect on his lyrics. David understood that his praise was representative of his faith and trust in God. Psalm 118:14, "The Lord is my strength and my song, and He has become my salvation." One of the keys to deliverance is through our praise of God. Jeremiah 17:14, "Heal me, O Lord, and I shall be healed; save me, and I shall be saved: for thou art my praise." Psalms 106:12 says, "They believed they His words; they sang His praise." Praise is a declaration of your belief in what God is capable of doing or has promised already to do. Everything you utter in praise is the very thing you declare in your faith and belief. What you praise is what you believe.

King Jehoshaphat did the same thing when preparing for battle against the armies of Edom. The first step he took was recognizing he needed help from God. He knew he couldn't do it on his own, but he trusted that God was powerful enough to fill the gap of his weakness. His step one: he humbled his heart and trusted God. The Spirit of God honored his humility and sent him a message through a fellow member of Israel. The messenger said in 2 Chronicles 20:17, "You will not have to fight this battle. Stand firm. You will see how the Lord will save you. Do not lose hope. Go out and face them tomorrow. The Lord be with you."

When Jehoshaphat heard this, he trusted that God was already working on his behalf. He then took step 2: he saw and believed through his kingdom lens and gave praise. The next morning, he went out with appointed Levites singing praises with loud voices. They continued to sing and waited on the Lord. By the time they arrived on the battlefield, their enemies were fighting each other, and the majority were dead when Jehoshaphat and his army arrived. That's right; the battle was already won! It was like their praises ignited the reflection of what they saw in Spirit, and it brought it to pass on Earth. The faith and confessions of praise were made pleasing to God, and He provided. Again, what you shout in praise is what you believe in faith. Praise is a powerful weapon!

Praise is also a sweet savor to God. Scriptures seem to reflect that it turns His anger away. Usually, when people hear "anger of the Lord," they get such a negative perception of God's character. How I compare this to God is thinking about how I parent my kids. They do things all the time that make me angry. You just want what's best for them. You want to protect them. You want them to be the most successful they could ever be. However, they don't always see the full picture like you see and have experienced. They become rebellious, and it angers you. The one thing that will turn your anger is them coming to you with a heart full of love, respect, and willingness to trust your advice. When they do this, they confess their faith and trust in your parenting. That's what praise does for God. It turns His anger. Isaiah 12:1, "And in that day thou shalt say, O Lord, I will praise thee: though thou wast angry with me, thine anger is turned away and thou comfortedst me." Later on, in verses 4—6, it explains His favor was released because the inhabitants started to praise and thank Him for all of His excellent deeds. In doing so, they declared their love for Him.

I believe that the courageous and trusting role of those who are appointed as "Levites," will help produce peace among the people. The book of Revelation also reflects this thought. Even a book many people regard as something to fear reflects such a powerful representation of peace and victory. Remember, we have to choose to look through the Father's lens that always gives life and renewal for good. When the shout of praise is heard, Jesus is brought forth. Anytime unified voices lift their praises to the Lord, victory is declared, the presence of the Lord appears. Jesus loves to show His power amid our praise. In Revelation 14:1—3, Jesus appeared during the praising of the 144,000. In Revelation 19:5, "Praise our God, all ye His servants, and ye that fear Him, both small and great." Right after this, in verse 11, heaven opened, and Jesus appeared with the rest of His army. Praise typically precedes the glory and physical representation of victory in Jesus. The praise was heard before He appeared. In 2 Chronicles 19:10 & 11, praise is what Jehoshaphat instructed the Levites to tell the rest of the Israelites to do. They said to the people that if you trust in the Lord, nothing will trespass against you. In verse 11, it says that the Levites were described as being "officers before them." They "deal courageously, and the Lord is with them." When we see through our flesh lens, of course, we will see doom and death, but if we trust in the Lord and see through His lens, we will see into the heavenly realm of life and peace. We will see our eternal life with Him and not be afraid. That's what I think Hebrews 7:22—25 says when we draw close with God. When we learn His ways and His protection, we walk in full trust with Him. We are made intercessors for others with Jesus. Verse 25 says, "to the uttermost that come unto God by Him, seeing He ever liveth to make intercession for them." We are appointed to bring comfort to those who fear the destruction. The more I've gotten to know the peace of the

Father, the more I view His protection and purpose of life for me.

When you get to know Him, you understand that even His fire is meant to produce life. His consuming fire is a way to purify me, making me a new creation in Him. That's why I believe Paul and Tychicus preached on comforting hearts to trust the Father and rest in the hope of what the Father's fire can bring. He turns it for His good. When we praise amid trial, turmoil, and what seems like destruction, His mercy shines through. He covers those who trust Him and choose to see Him through a life-giving lens because that's who He is. His covering protects us. 2 Chronicles 7:3, "And when all the children of Israel saw how the fire came down, and the glory of the Lord upon the house, they bowed themselves with their faces to the ground upon the pavement, and worshipped, and praised the Lord, saying, For He is good; for His mercy endureth forever."

I think that's also why the story of Shadrach, Meshach, and Abednego is essential as well. It teaches us to not fear the fire that may appear during times of tribulation. God is with us as He was with them. The fiery furnace was the thing that proved the power of God's glory to King Nebuchadnezzar. And the King's magicians and astrologers couldn't replicate or explain it. Sounds familiar to the times, right?

Going through the fire is the true test of our faith to trust that He will save and renew. That's what we are called to show others. The kingdom that stands confident in His protection will remain. Others who don't know Him will try to run and escape Him. But, Isaiah 33:14—17 says, "The sinners in Zion are afraid; fearfulness hath surprised the hypocrites. Who among us shall dwell with the devouring fire? Who among us shall dwell with everlasting burnings? He that walketh righteously…Thine eyes shall see the king in his beauty: they shall behold the land that is very far off." God's faithful see through their "kingdom lens." They are not shaken. The church in the midst of Zion is called to comfort those who fear. Psalms 125:1, "They that trust in the Lord shall be as mount Zion, which cannot be removed, but abideth forever. As the mountains are round about Jerusalem, so the Lord is round about His people from henceforth even forever." Satan is trying to bring doubt to God's children. He's TRYING to shake up Zion. He can't.

The foundation WILL NOT BE REMOVED. Don't let him convince you that it can. He lies to you because He knows that the building up of people trusting in the Lord will bring the appearance of God's glory. When that happens, it's all over for him. Psalms 102:16, "When the Lord shall build up Zion, He shall appear in His glory." We must trust the Father. All we have to do is stand firm and declare His power through our praise.

I think that's why Jesus is referred to as the Prince of Peace for the time of harvest and gathering of people who will believe. He was the peace offering sacrifice on the Cross for the lost. Which is also what I think another meaning of the Scripture "to suffer is to know Christ" alludes to in (1 Peter 4:13). That's why it says to rejoice and consider it joy when we face trials (James 1:2—4) because through those moments, His glory will be revealed. It's hard to be patient and trust in a seemingly disastrous situation. However, trials and testing are the ultimate proving of our faith. The trial is what the devil is using to distract you from what God has for you. It's up to us to realize the power that Jesus has given us when we choose to accept it. His defeat over Satan happened on the Cross. When we allow Satan's torment to overcome us, we have not entirely accepted the power given to us by Christ. If we did, we wouldn't let the devil win, EVER. We wouldn't fear. Jesus is the Prince of Peace. Peace triumphs over the trial. We just have to believe it and walk in it.

Those who trust the life, goodness, victory, and saving grace of Jesus will praise before, during, and after tribulation. Wherever and whenever He has called us to be, we are to stand firm and wait on Him. Our patience is a testing of our faith. The tribulation, even the one discussed in the book of Revelation, stands as a test for people to grow in faith in Him. Christ does not call for His children to crumble. He calls for us to live in joyous triumph from the beginning (Genesis) till the end (Revelation). We just have to choose to believe and open our eyes to the victory in and through Christ. That's the whole premise behind Revelation. It's God's "revelation" to us of His restoration. He's not looking to destroy the Earth, but to RESTORE the Earth. We must stop allowing the lies of the enemy to tell us otherwise. I feel that the last trumpet sound mentioned in Revelation is the shout of praise by the voices of those who see His redemption and purifying of the old made new.

Isaiah 58:1 says, "Lift up thy voice like a trumpet." Psalms 30:11, "Thou hast turned for me my mourning into dancing: thou hast put off my sackcloth, and girded me with gladness."

Comfort those who go through the fire, because amid the wrath to remove the torment is mercy. Show them that standing firm and trusting the Lord will be the ultimate cleansing of our flesh and the Earth as we know it. 1 Peter 4:12 and 13, "Beloved, think not strange concerning the fiery trial which is to try you, as though some strange thing happened to you: But rejoice, inasmuch as ye are partakers of Christ's sufferings; that, when His glory shall be revealed, ye may be glad also with exceeding joy." His fire burns away old flesh and doubt so people can call on the Savior to enter His kingdom. I believe that the time of tribulation will be a place of trusting through the fire. It's the testing of the faith of those who remain and a calling forth of souls to enter into His kingdom. The gathering of people outside of the gates of His new kingdom will be a place of glorious sacrificial praise. The sacrifice of old flesh and sinful ways to be burned away and waxed old like a garment through the sounds of shouts of praise. I believe that the glory of Jesus shining through us will be an outpouring to those who fear. The fear of torment will transform into the fear of the Lord. The godly fear through the revelation of how great His power is. Proverbs 16:6, "By mercy and truth iniquity is purged: and by the fear of the Lord men depart from evil." When we learn how to live by seeing through the perspective of Christ, we will demonstrate love and truth to others that leads them to the awestruck wonder of God's power, the same power that saves their souls from the destruction of the fire. They will see that they are meant for life with Him and not to be appointed to die in the destruction of the evil.

He gave me a vision recently of smoke. I kept seeing smoke float up and to stay low and stable to avoid it. He told me that the burning is the releasing of the bad spirits of torment. It's causing the ways and memory of the wicked to go away. Even during the time that the book of Revelation reveals. What we view as wrath has a purpose. God uses it as a way for Him to give comfort to us and encourage us to trust Him even if people have to face the fire. I believe that's what Revelation 14 could be referring to in the Scripture. Verses 12 & 13 say, "Here is the patience of the saints: here are they that keep the commandments of God, and the faith of Jesus. Blessed are the dead which die in the Lord from henceforth: Yea, saith the Spirit, that they may rest from their labours; and their works do follow them." Those who trust in the Lord don't fear the fire and see it as destruction. If it's from Him, and we believe and trust in Him, then He is good to those who believe it. He is with us. Comfort those who fear the fire that is to come. Tell them to cry out to the one who saves. I think that's why verse 15 says, "And another angel came out of the temple, crying with a loud voice to Him that sat on the cloud, thrust in thy sickle and reap: for the time is come for thee to reap; for the harvest of the Earth is ripe." The sickle is used to gather the wheat. I genuinely feel like this could be a place where Jesus is continuing to save souls from the fire of destruction. When you place your trust and patience in Him no matter what you face, He will pull you out. Those who trust in His saving power, praise Him in the midst of chaos. And, I believe that the believers are witnessing what is taking place here in Revelation. They see it happening, but they are out of the way of destruction. They are calling out to those still amid tribulation to trust in the One who is reaching out to save. The saints praise in the victory of His justice, but also in the saving grace of rescuing souls. We declare in faith His wondrous power. Psalms 132:7, "We will go into His tabernacles: we will worship at His footstool."

Victory over the enemy was established through the expression of praise from the beginning of Scripture to the end. The Bible ends with an amazing visual of the gathering of all to praise and shout with overwhelming joy. All of us will be gathered at His footstool to worship Him. His glory and His mercy are everlasting. Malachi 3:2, "Who may abide the day of His coming? And who shall stand when He appeareth? For He is like a refiner's fire, and like fullers' soap." Those who trust in the Lord don't fear, they praise. They praise for the victory that is promised, and for the souls that are being saved. Don't be afraid of the fire—stand firm. Trust in Him. He died on the Cross and was resurrected to bring life for those who choose Him; all you have to do is believe. Praise His name forever because He has given you the victory.

• CHAPTER 11 •

The Day of Harvest

I'm finally writing this chapter. I've been looking forward to getting to this point to tell you one of the most powerful visions that God gave to me months back. It is such a message of hope and victory it makes me want to jump out of my skin, run down the street, and shout out how amazing our God is.

One night I was lying in bed just praising and thanking Him for considering me worthy enough to show me all of these things. It was the same night He showed me the vision that taught me how to look past the wall of distraction to focus on Him. As I realized the power I have to overcome the enemy, I saw something incredible. The first thing that appeared was an "X" shape. I heard "target" and "'X' marks the spot." The "X" then appeared in the middle of a square. The square then was inside another larger square, and it kept going until I realized I had an aerial view looking down on top of a pyramid. I understood this to be an altar, and I knew I was in Egypt. It could very well have been the Great Pyramid. Anyway, all of a sudden, the shape of a cross slammed onto the top of the pyramid. As soon as it hit, I heard and saw an explosive boom. I didn't see the pyramid crumble, but all I could see was a fireball burning amongst it. Next, I saw a row of thousands of soldiers lined up facing the same direction, all sitting atop white horses. They wore pointed helmets and armor of gold, which stood out to me. It was so beautiful and shiny. They just stood there, tall and upright, not moving. It was as if they were floating on top of the pyramid.

The next thing that I recognized were tombs upon tombs all connected and tunneled among each other beneath the ground below. Suddenly, each grave exploded in a cloud. One after another, "boom, boom, boom, boom." I was laying there awestruck at what was taking place. Then out of nowhere, and I kid you not, my right arm started to raise. I can't explain what was happening. It was as if the rest of my body was paralyzed. I didn't know why just my right arm was moving. I was in disbelief and even tried to raise my left arm, but I couldn't do it.

As my right arm lifted, I began to chant, "Rise up, Rise up, Rise up, Rise up" over and over. I then heard the word "venerated" over and over. Side note venerated is the highest form of exaltation. As I was saying, "rise up," I heard other voices join me. Then more and more graves exploded, causing many more soldiers to rise out of them. I immediately had a sense in my heart that they were armies and men that use to be against God. The moment I knew that I heard God say, "It's all for me. I've turned them all for me." I started freaking out on the inside. I felt such an omnipotent presence that I couldn't help but shout myself. As my spirit shouted what felt like the loudest roar possible, others shouted with me. It almost caused everything to shake. I remember trying to look around for the evil to come against us. I saw the armor and the prep for battle, but I never did see anything come up against us. It was like it had all went away. Within a moment, every evil had gone out.

Immediately, it was as if my spirit got transported into a New Jerusalem. I saw a city in a bowl shape. I know this sounds weird, but all I can describe it as is a never-ending bowl. I was flying all around in it, and the buildings went up into the bowl-shaped walls, and it just kept going. I remember seeing a glowing light in the center. Then I saw Jesus on the side of it. He was smiling at me. I was soaring all around, and I wanted to go toward Him. I remember saying, "I want to go frolic with Jesus." It was as if I was in some fairy tale land. I was so happy and flying everywhere. I could even make myself transform into a giant version of myself every time I would say, "The joy of the Lord is my strength." Boom! I would shoot up in a giant form and back down again. I was flying and laughing with Jesus. I don't remember anyone else being there, but Him and I.

I was so happy that I began to cry, but as soon as tears would come to my eyes, they evaporated into the air. It was like it became food for God. I don't know why I understood it like that at the time, but I did. I knew I had to go back down again. As I floated back down to Earth, I saw that the city of Jerusalem fell slowly with me. The foundations of it and the bowl shape flattened out over the planet. Right before it laid out, I heard a sizzling sound behind me. I turned to see a giant wall that looked like a dam. Okay, when I say this, please don't think I'm a whack-a-doodle. The bottom of the dam had an opening that looked like a vagina. I know, I know, that sounds so insane and weird, but here's why. Out of it were flowing streams of water. They were streams of living water, which is why I believe it was shaped like that—a hint to let me know that the waters released life. I then heard, "Love. Love covers all sin." Its stream poured out on everything and everyone. I snapped out of the vision. At the time, I didn't understand. I remember thinking, "Wait a second, will He turn the evil armies for Him"?? I was so confused.

In the days that followed, I kept seeing the significance of the transition from the numbers 6 to 7. I kept seeing them over and over again. I remembered that man was created on the sixth day, and God's holy day is the seventh. There are many themes in the Bible of the transition from 6 to 7. Deliverance is always done either on day or year 7. Six is made new on seven. Numbers 31:23, "Everything that may abide the fire, ye shall make it go through the fire, and it shall be clean: nevertheless, it shall be purified with the water of separation: and all that abideth not the fire ye shall make go through the water. And ye shall wash your clothes on the seventh day, and ye shall be clean, and afterward, ye shall come into the camp." The fire through the heavenly lens is purifying to those who trust Him. It refines the old flesh man. Jesus rescues those who trust in Him from the fire of tribulation and leads them into the waters of life (Revelation 7:14, paraphrased). His love covers as His blood cleanses and the waters of life wipe away all the tears of suffering. That's what's so beautiful about the imagery of the cloud and rainbow at His throne (Revelation 4:3—5). It's symbolic of His promise to us that His will is to save representing His covenant of grace, mercy, peace, and reconciliation with humanity.

He keeps showing me that the clean, new body is made whole on the seventh day, from six to seven, like a rebirth of His goodness on His holy Sabbath. I believe He's showing me this to demonstrate breaking the curse of man's old flesh that Satan corrupted, which was created on day six. God redeemed and reversed the curse of the enemy when

Jesus died on the Cross. Jesus finished His work and claimed His victory. His return in Revelation will bring about the restoration of all things in full form in the natural for the inhabitants of the Earth to see. He's coming to fulfill His completed work that He accomplished on the Cross. Revelation 18:8 says that the plagues upon the evil will "come in one day." The fire will purify the Earth. To remove the evil that is tormenting it.

Right after this, Revelation gives a visual of the Marriage Supper of the Lamb. It's a celebration of Christ's people overcoming the old to gain new life with Him in heaven, which appears to be the beginning of the "thousand-year reign with Christ" (Revelation 20:4). Then in Revelation 21:1-2, John sees the New Jerusalem descending down to Earth. I kept feeling in my spirit that the old would be made new in a matter of a day. I really don't think the completed harvest is going to be some long drawn out thing. It's like the nation of Israel, which was born in one day just as was prophesied in Isaiah 66:8. Also, I want to point out, what if the "thousand-year reign with Christ" as believed after the Tribulation is reflective of what 2 Peter 3:8 says, "But, beloved be not ignorant of this one thing, that one day is with the Lord as a thousand years, and a thousand years as one day"? Maybe that's why Scriptures say Satan's last rebellion is brief once he is loosed from the pit for a "short season" after the Millennial Reign of Christ's kingdom. What if the vision the Holy Spirit gave me is correct? What if the quickening of the flesh and the establishment of New Jerusalem will happen in one day? The symbolism from six to seven? It seems like it could be possible. We shall see! In fact, the night I had the vision was right around midnight from the 26th to the 27th; there's that number six to seven again. Other visions I had similar to this were always from the 6th to the 7th, which I never noticed until I looked back on my journaling. It was crazy! God never failed to amaze me and prove Himself to me.

God is wanting to give us His perspective of Revelation. That's why He calls it the book of REVELATION. It's Him revealing to us HIS perspective. Those who choose Him will not ultimately suffer but triumph in Him. Why? Because Jesus won the battle over Satan already. I believe that people will be gathered for a prepared battle. They are expecting to go to war with each other. Satan brings them together. Those who are secure in Christ and understand His ways, trust that they will not have to fight. The battle was won on the Cross, and Satan is defeated, but he still desires to confuse many. He will twist the truth. People will think that they are to go to war. However, according to God's promise, we don't have to. Just know, the people who stand firm and wait on the Lord are the ones who overcome. That's why Saul got fussed at by Samuel in 1 Samuel 13. He took the battle in his own hands and killed all the people instead of waiting on the Lord. Jesus promises us the battle has already been won. It took place on the Cross. Revelation 17:14 says, "These shall make war with the Lamb, and the Lamb shall overcome them." Overcome doesn't have to mean that a fight will take place necessarily. Remember what I said earlier about the brightness of God's glory will defeat the Wicked one? The sword of His mouth, I believe is the shout of praise of the Word of God from His saints. It's the declaration of His Word and authority over the enemy. We have victory in the power of His Word and the appearance of His Second Coming. And, the wicked will be judged by Jesus, the Word made flesh, who releases justice based on His Word. God's statues stand forever.

Once the Lamb of God appears, His glory will cause all to bow. That's how everyone will know who the One true King is. The foretelling of this victory is reflected over and over all throughout the Bible. The head of the serpent in the Garden, Satan, has been crushed. I can't wait for that to happen. Miracles will take place. Righteousness will be known, and restoration will be complete. His Second Coming is so close, I can feel it. Can you picture that day? Close your eyes, imagine the turning of the wicked, and all the pain and suffering of the world vanished away. The one TRUE King and Savior coming to set up His kingdom and righteousness as He takes back what the enemy has stolen.

The devil wants to make us think we are to fight a horrendous and horrible battle. He's going to gather everyone that he can. It's going to require a lot of hard work and deceiving on his part. That's why I believe God allows Antichrist to arise. Because the unbelievers are not choosing to see life with God, He allows Satan to come upon them to continue to deceive them. It's because they choose to see the lies of Satan and are blinded from life. I think God allows this so they can be brought to the battle with the righteous. It's so He can fulfill His plan. God needs a way to gather them even if that means He uses Satan to do it. This is where I believe the infamous "hour of temptation" comes in to play. For one hour, people will be confused. Well, everyone except those who have given their lives to Christ. I believe that the biggest indicator to tell who the one true God is, He's the one who stands firm. Just like the horseman in my vision. They're prepped, they're ready. However, they know what the Word of the Lord has said to them. "The battle is already won." Ephesians 6:13, "Wherefore take unto you the whole armor of God, that ye may be able to withstand in the evil day, and having done all, to stand." 2 Thessalonians 2:8, "And then shall that Wicked be revealed, whom the Lord shall consume with the Spirit of his mouth, and shall destroy with the brightness of His coming." I believe that we who trust in Him have a powerful part to play. Our shouts of victory and our praise can release the consuming fire of His glory. Again, when the ways of the enemy are destroyed before the people, everyone will know who the One true God is. There won't have to be a battle. I love later what is said to the church in verse 13 and 14, "But we are bound to give thanks always to God for you, brethren beloved of the Lord, because God hath from the beginning chosen you to salvation through sanctification of the Spirit and belief of the truth: Whereunto He called you by our gospel. To the obtaining of the glory of our Lord Jesus Christ." I believe that when we release our praise, the blinders of the enemy will go away, and they will see the truth and their salvation. Jesus is life-giving, all-powerful, loving, and merciful to those who cry out in faith to Him. How much more of His glory will be revealed when even the enemies turn toward Him!

I want to go back to my vision and show you some Scriptures that God showed me after I made sense of it all. So, remember when I said I saw it all happening over a pyramid in Egypt? I think this is symbolic because it's the place in the Bible where God delivered His people. His people always came out of Egypt before they were led into the Promised Land. It's where He promised that He would turn back His enemies. Hosea 1:10 and 11, "It shall come to pass, that in the place where it was said unto them, Ye are not my people, there it shall be said unto them, Ye are the sons of the living God. Then all the children of Judah and the children of Israel be gathered together, and appoint themselves one head and they shall come up out of the land." I believe this is where God will utterly deliver His people who are being held captive on the Earth by the strongholds of Satan. Isaiah 61:1, "He hath sent me to bind up the brokenhearted to proclaim liberty to the captives, and the opening of the prison to them that are bound; To proclaim the acceptable year of the Lord, and the day of vengeance of our God; to comfort all that mourn." His "vengeance" is to take back what has been stolen from Him, His creation. These Scriptures are a foretelling of Jesus and what He would do to set in motion what God planned from the beginning, a mighty harvest and gathering of all who would believe in Him (Hosea 6:11).

Hosea 13:4, "Yet I am the Lord thy God from the land of Egypt, and thou shalt know no god but me: for there is no savior beside me." Now you may ask, God is from Egypt?? I think this is symbolic of everything He has done there for His people. Who knows, maybe in this area, in a hidden realm, the Garden of Eden does lie in "Egypt." Many clues throughout Scripture could lead to that as well, which could also make sense because anything that the enemy has taken over (Egypt is one area he has) was initially stolen from God. I believe when the devil is drawn to something, that means it's important. Scriptures reflect that Egypt is a special land that is part of the land that is promised to be claimed back. I know this may sound strange since the entire Earth is the Lord's and He will heal and redeem it in it's entirety. But, Egypt spiritually represents a lot of the world today as well. Our economy, entertainment, false beliefs, etc. I have had visions of more restoration and taking back in that land. There's something very significant about it that He is showing me. Like the Scriptures in Isaiah 19:19—25, "In that day shall there be an altar to the Lord in the midst of the land of Egypt, and a pillar at the border thereof to the Lord. And it shall be for a sign and for a witness unto the Lord of hosts in the land of Egypt: for they shall cry unto the Lord because of the oppressors, and He shall send them a savior, and a great one, and He shall deliver them. And the Lord shall be known to Egypt, and the Egyptians shall know the Lord in that day, and shall do sacrifice and oblation; yea they shall vow and vow unto the Lord, and perform it. And the Lord shall smite Egypt: he shall smite and heal it: and they shall return even to the Lord and He shall be entreated of them and shall heal them. In that day shall there be a highway out of Egypt to Assyria, and the Assyrian shall come into Egypt, and the Egyptian into Assyria, and the

Egyptians shall serve with the Assyrians. In that day shall Israel be the third with Egypt and with Assyria, even a blessing in the midst of the land: whom the Lord of hosts shall bless, saying, Blessed be Egypt my people, and Assyria the work of my hands, and Israel mine inheritance." I saw it exactly like this in my vision. It was so incredible.

He even showed me over and over in Scripture why my right hand lifted as I shouted: "rise up." The right arm is symbolic of the side that saves. Psalms 98:1 is a prime example of this, "O sing unto the Lord a new song; for He hath done marvelous things: His right hand, and His holy arm, hath gotten Him the victory." Psalms 118:16—23 as well, "The right hand of the Lord is exalted: the right hand of the Lord doeth valiantly. I shall not die, but live, and declare the works of the Lord. This gate of the Lord into which the righteous shall enter. The stone which the builders rejected is become the head stone of the corner. This is the Lord's doing; it is marvelous in our eyes." I have two things to say about this Scripture. First, THE RIGHT ARM DECLARES THE SAVING OF HIS PEOPLE! And, second, the stone that the builders rejected, do you know that the Great Pyramid in Egypt is missing the top capstone? No one knows why they didn't finish building that piece. I believe God knew this and used that for a symbol for those who are searching. Don't let the enemy confuse you into thinking that the world belongs to him. I believe God has always used Egypt as an example. The Illuminati, highest degree Free Masons, and other secret society groups want to claim the land there for Lucifer. I don't think so!! Everything is God's. He is taking it back!

I believe that God is using His remnant, the body of Christ, to make way for the Head (Jesus) to redeem and turn the lost back to Him. By faith, I believe my God can do it! Hebrews 11:33 and 34 says, "Who through faith subdued kingdoms, through righteousness, obtained promises, stopped the mouths of lions, quenched the violence of fire, escaped the edge of the sword, out of weakness were made strong, waxed valiant in fight, turned flight the armies of the aliens." I think that the last line is so compelling and so hilarious. It's God's way of letting His humor show a little bit. He knew way before that the last days would have all sorts of alien talk. Guess what, my faith is that God is going to make the "aliens" bow before Him. Those who haven't obtained mercy will see mercy. Those who haven't seen His glory will sure as heck see His glory. 1 Kings 8:41-43, "Concerning the stranger, that is not of thy people Israel, but cometh out of a far country for thy name's sake; For they shall hear of thy great name, and of thy strong hand, and of thy stretched out arm (probably the right one ha!) when he shall come and pray toward this house; Hear thou in heaven thy dwelling place, and do according to all that the stranger calleth to thee for: that all people of the Earth may know thy name." You see that???

I believe we are not to "smite" our enemies and doom them to destruction when given a chance at any point during the last days. It's God's choice who He wants to save, and He gave that power to Jesus. That's what I feel John 5:22 is reflective of when it says, "For the Father judgeth no man, but hath committed all judgment unto the Son." We are not called to repay evil with evil (1 Peter 3:8—10). We are called to respond with life and love, just as Jesus did. Those who come against us haven't experienced the goodness of God because they've been covered with Satan's lies. So, we should show them Christ's goodness. 2 Kings 6:22, "Thou shalt not smite them: wouldest though smite those whom thou hast taken captive with thy sword and with thy bow?

Set bread and water before them that they may eat and drink, and go to their master." When we ask for a redemption of souls, even for the souls of our enemies, we make way for Jesus to release spiritual rain over them. We call these things forth through the declaration of our praise, as we stand in faith, believing it will be done. Remember my waters of life visual? LOVE COVERS ALL. God is love, and He is always ready to save. I genuinely believe that we, the church, should work with Jesus to intercede for the salvation of souls from now till the end of the Tribulation. We are also the oil (because the Levites were in charge of the oil). We are to pour out the oil of our praise, the tears of our joy, over all the people. I believe that the "oil" of our praise and tears of joy are presented to Jesus, and it becomes an overflow to be poured out unto all as He sweeps across them.

Jeremiah 33:11, "The voice of joy, and the voice of gladness, the voice of the bridegroom, and the voice of the bride, the voice of them that shall say, Praise the Lord of hosts: for the Lord is good; for His mercy endureth for ever: and of them that shall bring the sacrifice of praise into the house of the Lord. For I will cause the return of the captivity of the land, as at the first, saith the Lord." God will honor our praise. In 1 Kings 20:42 He says, "Because thou hast let go out of thy hand a man whom I appointed to utter destruction, therefore thy life shall go for his life, and thy people for his people."

The moment we stop trying to take vengeance on those who come against us and call for the saving of their life is the moment we get into agreement with God's plan for the harvest. I believe that it will be the moment God will bring forth Jesus and His new kingdom. He's calling for a day of harvest. That time is now.

Going back to my first dream about the flooding Jordan River. Joshua 3:15 says that the river only floods during the time of harvest. We can't be afraid to step into a flood. He's calling us to renew and refresh our souls. He's calling us to a deeper relationship with Him right now. He's calling us to wake up, rise up, tune in to what He's saying, and get into the water to swim in the goodness of what He has given to us and those around us. In 2 Kings 5:14, the prophet instructed Naaman how to be healed of leprosy saying, "Then went he down and dipped himself SEVEN times in Jordan, according to the saying of the man of God: and his flesh came again like unto the flesh of a little child, and he was clean." God is asking us to trust Him. The fire and the waters look scary. That's exactly what the lens of destruction will tell you. Put on your kingdom lens so you can see like God sees. When you do that, the kingdom will come down. Harvest time is here.

• CHAPTER 12 •

Calling Down Heaven

Jeremiah 1:12, "Then the Lord said to me, 'You have seen well, for I am ready to perform My word.'" This verse comes from a dialogue between God and Jeremiah, as He taught Jeremiah how to see with His kingdom lens. When you read the Scriptures above this verse, you can see Jeremiah's humble character being expressed before the Lord. He didn't consider himself worthy of being used, but he trusted that God was there, and he heard and saw Him through spiritual eyes. Jeremiah was humble yet lacked doubt. That's the exact recipe of personality traits in people that God loves to use for His kingdom work. These traits also allowed Jeremiah to see the vision that God showed him. When you see the kingdom vision God has for you, it enables you to step forward with confidence and security. Even death will have no hold on you. The intentions and heart of the Father want to give you an overflow of the blessings of heaven. We don't have to wait for a new kingdom for those blessings to be released. We have access to His kingdom and blessings now. But to receive we have to believe. I believe God is waiting for us to realize that. That's when I think the new heavens and new Earth will come forth. You see, God loves for us to choose. As we trust and put our life in His hands, He hands authority right back to us. He doesn't force Christ or His kingdom on anyone. He wants us to have the freedom to choose it.

The more intense events become here on Earth, and the more Satan uses people against God's plans and people, the more I want to draw nearer to God, who has given me a brand new outlook on these "last days." Growing up, I was almost fearful of the return of the Lord. Every church I grew up in emphasized the imminency of what those days may look like in the world. It was like fearmongering. Yes, His return is imminent. Yes, we are to fear the Lord, but the fear of the Lord is also comforting at the same time. It does not fear Him as destructive, but establishes a reverent awe of His power in us. God's presence is a mix of overwhelming, uncontrollable joy as well as an incomprehensible great-ness. He is so powerful that you can hardly withstand to be in the midst of Him, but when you are in that place, it's the most incredible feeling.

Often, we fear things we cannot fathom or comprehend. In that fear, however, for those who genuinely get to know His kindness, is joy, a feeling I want to share with people. That feeling will produce a humility in you that will impress people to draw near to Him. People who walk in that place will look at others through the eyes of love and the supernatural power of His grace. His goodness is something I would never want to be without, no matter what. I don't like to portray these days as something to fear. The kind of fear that fears destruction brings on torment. It's giving the destruction power over you. Godly fear is much different. Faith and trust in Christ bring life. He IS life. Focus on Christ to come, not the destruction to come. What you focus on is what you empower.

I used to look at the Rapture and entering His kingdom as events that seemed so far away. I didn't realize that I was keeping His kingdom at arm's length. I even feared the concept of the Rapture because I didn't want to lose anything that I had. I didn't want people that I loved to be left behind. God knows the desires of our hearts. He knows what brings us joy and comfort. I was so focused on what man's perspective of the Rapture and Tribulation was, that I wasn't drawing near to God so He could give me His perspective on it. The more I tuned into His promises and His comforting peace through Scripture and the voice of His Holy Spirit, the more He gave me a kingdom lens. He allowed me to see and feel what heaven would be like to such a degree that He placed it inside of me. He will do that for all of us. When He is in us, heaven resides in us as well. When you genuinely feel a connection with Him, it feels like you are finally home. There's no longer a fear of what you don't fully understand or know. You connect it to Earth and the people around you. The Rapture isn't viewed as a distant event since you're already walking and living in the presence of heaven by His Spirit. You no longer walk in fear of possible destruction or of any sort of tribulation either. You feel that connection of heaven so strongly that you want to share that power, joy, and fulfillment with everyone around you, which is exactly what He's calling the church to feel and do.

He's calling the church to show others. People around you are not destined to be left behind according to the Father, so show them there's a prepared way through faith in Christ.

If Christians end up going through the Tribulation, we have no reason to fear. If we believe in Christ, His full power is within us. His power is over any destruction, even the destruction of the Great Tribulation to come. God is always in control. The destiny of destruction only belongs to evil, not those who choose Christ. Accepting Him as Savior, is precisely that, to be saved from destruction. The power of God's presence should be our focus. His promises say that He will not hurt the "oil and wine" (Revelation 6:6). The oil and wine are those who believe and accept Him, those who choose to utilize His goodness. Remember, the Levites oversaw the oil and wine. They ushered in the presence of the Lord. Whoever believes His promises, He will keep a hedge of protection over and around them. He's calling us to lead others to trust in Him so they can have peace and security as well.

Think of the story of Jesus sleeping on the boat during the storm. Everyone on the vessel was freaking out. They were looking for an escape from what appeared to be certain death because the storm looked impossible to survive. They trusted that Jesus would provide the escape, which is why they went to Him. However, Jesus was aggravated with them because they feared from the start. If we truly trust and believe He will not hurt the "oil and wine" in these days, then we shouldn't allow ourselves to look at the potential harm in these days through the lens of fear. The victors are the ones who face the battle standing firm, being unshakable and waiting on the Lord. His hand is over us; we must choose to see it.

Why are we so fearful of the Tribulation? Why do we shake when we hear things like Y2K, anthrax, hurricanes, earthquakes, atomic warfare, and Coronavirus? Yes, the Bible teaches us to be on the watch and ready, but that doesn't mean to focus on the fear of what those things will bring. Could those things bring harm? Yes, of course, they can bring harm. However, walking in full authority and faith teaches us that we possess a power greater than any of that. It's like we are walking contradictions when those things shake us. I'm not fearful of facing the tribulation because God promises us that through Him, our enemies will fall at our feet. Even if my natural body's time is up, I no longer fear the death of it. It's because it's not death. It's a transition from this life to a greater life.

Now, does that mean that God doesn't call us to prep for things here on Earth and utilize means of protection with material things? No, it does not. He can call us to do anything. The important thing, and the first step we have to consider is to seek the voice of His Holy Spirit. When we go to Him first, not out of fear, but in trust, He's going to guide us every step. He can communicate in any kind of way. We will know when it happens. He may speak audibly; He may use the voice of another, He may send someone to rescue you in time of need. It may look like anything or anyone. He may teach us to seek wisdom and research on how to handle certain things to overcome them. He might give us peace to stand still and wait. Look at the Israelites in the desert. Because of Moses' faithfulness, God sent a food supply down from heaven. He can even physically transport our bodies just like He did with Philip in Acts 8:39 and Enoch in Genesis 5:25! We do not need to worry when we've been given peace in Him. He makes the impossible, possible.

God plans to unite Earth and heaven once again, as He did in the beginning before the fall of man. The more people realize and activate the power of heaven within them, heaven is going to manifest in the natural. Remember, when we walk in the Spirit lens of heaven with Christ in us, our words and deeds make heaven reflect in the natural. What if Christ is waiting on us to become aware of His power in us to manifest Himself and His kingdom on Earth in the natural? Yes, His timing is established, so I'm not saying we decide what God does. His timing is already mapped out. However, it does mean that He has what He's going to do in us mapped out as well. My point is that He values us so much that He is using us to implement His plans and timing without us realizing it. We don't know when He will manifest His kingdom in the natural, but I believe that He is working in us to fulfill it all just like His intention for us to choose Him freely. He loves it when we implement His plans and purpose. Remember the Garden, Adam and Eve worked hand in hand with God. Though He was in control, God gave Adam responsibility for the things of the Earth. He valued us enough to put the keys of the kingdom of heaven and Earth right back in our hands when we walk according to His will.

Things on Earth may appear to get ugly. Wars, armies, fire, and threats will arise, but remember the prayers of David. "For this shall every one that is godly pray unto thee in a time when thou mayest be found: surely in the floods of great waters they shall not come nigh unto him. Thou art my hiding place thou shalt preserve me from trouble; thou shalt compass me about songs of deliverance, Selah." See that? David was utilizing the power of praise for God in time of deliverance. When things happen, praise Him. When fear tries to overcome you, throw on some praise music and declare your victory in Him. Declare your faith in the authority Jesus gave you over the enemy. Isaiah 43:2, "When you pass through the waters, I will be with you; and when you pass through the rivers, they will not sweep over you. When you walk through the fire, you will not be burned; the flames will not set you ablaze."

God is calling His church not to fear. It doesn't matter if we are raptured pre-tribulation, mid-tribulation, or post-tribulation, we shouldn't focus there. It's not His will for us to try to determine the timing anyway. If we're walking in His Spirit, we will feel immense pressing as He leads us and He will teach us the signs of the times giving us the information we need for every step. He will show us what we need to do and what we need to say to keep us and others from harm. If He's telling us to warn people of certain things, then He will give us peace to do so. And, when He does, it won't be out of fear. It will be with the desire to be prepared and trust in Him. We must be guided by His Spirit every step of the way. His will is for us to utilize all the power of heaven NOW. We have to pay close attention to His instructions and implement them as His Spirit guides us in each moment. That's what being ready means. He will lead us to share the goodness of His will and to save souls from the power of destruction.

We have power over the destruction that the enemy wants to bring on us and others. I believe God gives us the authority to help fulfill His will to show others that their destiny doesn't have to be overcome by destruction. Revelation doesn't say that all the people going through the Tribulation are going to be destroyed. It's only meant for Satan's demonic forces and those who blatantly choose him over Christ. I believe that the plagues and "wrath" of God during that time are supposed to stop evil from harming people. Just like God did with the Pharaoh in Egypt. He also uses it to bring people to repentance, to bring forth a humbling of hearts. His will is to save. It's not Him trying to BRING destruction, it's Him trying to STOP it. We can't change the fact that the destruction will come, but I believe that He has given us the authority to change people's pathways leading them out of evil and destruction. Right now, He is trying to awaken us to what He has already set in order.

God is with us; we must open our eyes to Him. If He protected Moses and the Israelites from the plagues, He would do it for us now. Even when it appears, there's no way to escape. That's why Moses was able to part the Red Sea. He listened to the voice of God and obeyed His instruction to the smallest detail. We, as believers, must teach by example. We must tune into the voice of God, especially these days with what is soon to come. Ignoring Him removes you from His comfort and protection. We must see from God's perspective through our kingdom lens. He is calling for an awakening in the church, that's more than just a positive self-help weekly session. It has to become a moment to moment encounter with His goodness, presence, and power.

It's not about what we can do to better ourselves, but what God will do through us for others. We can't just read Scripture, hear it, and decipher on our own what we should do about it. We have to dig deeper into learning the Word of God and the voice of the Holy Spirit to reveal the truth and application of it in our lives. Seek His kingdom FIRST (Matthew 6:33). Church should be where we learn to hear the voice of God and operate by the guidance of the Holy Spirit. Church is also a gathering of two or more people to see through the kingdom lens. Believers should all be encountering heaven on Earth in a more powerful way as we walk in the authority of the heavenly realm. There's something incredibly powerful about the unification of souls all drawing heaven down at once. It's like each person has their own spiritual rope to help pull down the kingdom of heaven. The more people that press in and pull-down God's presence, the more of His glory will press down on us. More people means greater heavenly presence. How do we do this? Praise, worship, prayer, etc. The modern construct of church cannot put limits on the presence of God. We can't keep Him in a box of constraints telling Him when, where, or how long He can show up. He shows up when we let go and let God. If we want His power to move in the church, we have to get out of the way and allow Him.

If we desire healing, if we need courage, if we want a deeper faith, we can't pull the reins back from allowing that to happen. Just because something we trusted and prayed for earlier didn't happen the way we expected it to, doesn't mean that God isn't real and doesn't answer when we call. It's all in His timing. He will provide, and when He does, He will give us His best which is above and beyond what we can ever imagine. Our trust in Him will give us the peace that keeps us strong until that happens. We persevere by trusting Him. It doesn't mean giving up when we face hardship or even death. Remember, death has no hold. Seeking Him through His Word and His voice will give you the kingdom lens to reveal that to you. Don't hold on to your life so tight that it gives you anxiety to lose it. Remember, Scripture says, "Whoever tries to save his life will lose it" (Luke 17:33). You don't have the answers on your own to know how to keep your life.

However, the Word says where you are weak, He is strong. Rest your weaknesses on Him. 2 Corinthians 12:9, "He has said to me, 'My grace is sufficient for you, for power is perfected in weakness.' Most gladly, therefore, I will rather boast about my weaknesses, so that the power of Christ may dwell in me." That Scripture is so awesome to me. His power is perfected in us when we persevere through our weaknesses. We can't let our weakness hold us back. It's not about what we CAN'T do, but what HE CAN do through us. Where you are incapable, He is capable.

If fear makes itself known in your life, because it will, recognize that it's because you still have doubt. I had to remind myself over and over that fear equals doubt. Overcoming fear takes practice. The moment fear presents itself inside of me, I say, "God, I cast my fear upon you. Where I am weak, you are strong. You haven't given me a spirit of fear, but of power, love, and a sound mind. You are my protection." When I practice declaring that out loud at that moment, a sense of peace surrounds me. Doubt slowly fades. The Prince of Peace is more powerful than the prince of the air, remember that. As you practice, as I did, your faith will grow.

God has commissioned His church to comfort the hurting and bring peace to those who fear. Isaiah 40:1 & 2, "Comfort ye, comfort ye my people, saith your God. Speak ye comfortably to Jerusalem, and cry unto her, that her warfare is accomplished, that her iniquity is pardoned: for she hath received of the Lord's hand double for all her sins." I refuse to let fear overtake me. His perfect love for me and in me, casts out ALL fear (1John 4:15). Where we must grow is our PERFECT love for Him, fear is the result of an unperfected love in me. My full trust in His love understands that He is over me and in me, protecting me. He has made me ready to face anything. I say, "BRING IT ON!" Before you say, "Don't say that! You're going to cause destruction to come forth!" Know this; I DO NOT FEAR ANYTHING. THE POWER OF DESTRUCTION HAS NO POWER OVER ME. If it comes forth, I will stand in its face and say, "Get behind me, Satan." Whatever you fear, you give it power over your life. God is my power, and I KNOW He is more powerful than whatever comes against me. Whatever our days will look like, we have no reason to fear.

God has completely and radically changed my viewpoint on "tribulation." The more things that rise against me, the more

God's glory will be released. 2 Thessalonians 1:7, "And to you who are troubled rest with us, when the Lord Jesus shall be revealed from heaven with His mighty angels." 1John 4:4, "You are from God, little children, and have overcome them; because greater is He who is in you than he who is in the world." Revelation 3:21, "He who overcomes, I will grant to him to sit down with Me on My throne, as I also overcame and sat down with My Father on His throne." The more the enemy rises, the more the Father will rise above. As soon as they appear, I will declare the praise and power of the Lord Jesus Christ, my rock, and my salvation.

I see the loss of hope in people both outside and inside the church walls. The devil thinks He can destroy the foundations of the Father, but boy is he wrong. If you don't like the things happening around you, even in the church, don't walk away. What good are you doing for the kingdom by walking away? We are called to bring change, to be the hope, to be the example of His love and kindness. We are called to walk in the footsteps of Jesus. The Holy Spirit is in us and goes with us wherever we go. If there is a season where you have to step back for a bit to seek a deeper relationship with Christ, so be it. However, pray for those you step back from at that time. Don't give up on them. Be an intercessor for them and the kingdom. He's ready to renew and strengthen what He's started in you. Philippians 1:6, "Being confident of this, that He who began a good work in you will carry it on to completion until the day of Christ Jesus." You are needed for His kingdom. Don't let the lies of the enemy tell you that you don't have a part to play in bringing people to Him. Don't ever stop fighting. Don't ever stop caring or grow weary in doing good. You are created to persevere. Romans 15:13, "May the God of hope fill you with all joy and peace as you trust in Him, so that you may overflow with hope by the power of the Holy Spirit."

God wants you to draw near to Him so that He can draw near to you. He wants you to know His love for you. He wants to renew hope and strength in you. He wants to remove the doubt and confusion that contaminates your thoughts. His kingdom is waiting for you to lay hold of it by faith. I believe that's what Jesus meant in Matthew 10:7 when He said, "And as ye go, preach, saying, the kingdom of heaven is at hand." The actual Greek translation says, "draw near the heavens." He wasn't only saying the kingdom is coming soon; He was saying you have the power of the kingdom in you now. You can draw heaven near. Why? Because choosing Jesus, instills that within you. You walk in the full power of heaven. When you become one with the Father and develop a deep intimate relationship with Him, He shows you heaven.

I didn't always have these visions and dreams. They aren't specific to me. I'm not more special than you or anyone else. God gave dreams and visions to Abraham, Moses, Elijah, David, Paul, and many others, which didn't have to be for them alone either. They were just the ones willing, humble, and trusting. Their faith and reverence for the Father gave them the keys to unlock mysteries, a gift that is available to all. It's available to those who are hungry to know Christ more. Keep your pride in check, so you will be careful to see and hear Him. Humbling yourself is a moment to moment check-in. He has renewed something so incredible in me. My hope and mission are for all to feel what He has done for me because I know when that happens, their perspective of the world around them will change.

When you come to know God at a deeper level, He will make you feel so special. He will reveal the mysteries of the kingdom to you so you can bring comfort to others. I genuinely believe that's why He gave me these visions. Colossians 1:27, "To whom God would make known what is the riches of the glory of this mystery among the Gentiles; which is Christ in you, the hope of glory." He wants to speak to you. You are part of the Body of Christ with a mission to help comfort and save souls. You are valued, and He wants you to be a picture of heaven on Earth for all to see. Jeremiah 31:3, "Yes, I have loved you with an everlasting love; therefore, with lovingkindness, I have drawn you."

I waited way too long to seek Him deeper. If I had known a glimpse of what He's been showing me before now, I would have done this a long time ago. However, it's never too late. Just a moment with Him, makes all the moments I had without Him disappear.

If we want to see Jesus appear in all His full glory, we have to represent Him in spirit here on Earth. The only way to represent Him is to get to know Him. If we want the natural reflection of heaven on Earth, we have to reflect it in the spiritual first. It's going to take more than one person in Christ to fulfill and help implement His will of reuniting heaven here on Earth again. He's trying to awaken His people. He's calling for a revival gathering. I KNOW it's going to happen. My kingdom lens allows me to see that happen, and I will not stop sharing His goodness until it does.

God is trying to speak to those who are willing to listen. He's calling for an outpouring of His Spirit. This time is so crucial. He has pressed so heavily on me lately, and I know it is for a reason. We have to pay attention. We can't allow ourselves to be distracted by the busyness of life. We are called to something so much bigger than the regular cycles of everyday life. It's time for us to set our eyes on the things above, so we can reflect them here on Earth. I don't know about you, but I'm ready to see lives changed. I'm prepared to see oppression lifted off of people. I'm ready to see people walking in the love that they were created for in this life. The power of heaven is in our hands for us to use NOW. We are called to bring healing, restoration, hope, joy, and salvation. Look at what Jesus did when He walked on the Earth. Everything He did, He has appointed us to do. We are the hands and feet of Jesus because He has called us His body (1Corinthians 12:27). He's calling for us all to be in unified agreement and authority of it. Ephesians 1:10, "As a plan for the fullness of time, to unite all things in him, things in heaven and things on Earth." If we know and can visualize heaven to be all glorious and all victorious, it's time we walk in His will for it to be present here on Earth as well. He wants us to live in full assurance and peace NO MATTER WHAT WE FACE. We are created for so much more than what we see for ourselves. His goodness goes beyond our comprehension. It's time to rise up and be like the Levites. Let's bring down the full presence of heaven. Matthew 6:10, "Thy kingdom come. Thy will be done in Earth, as it is in heaven."

Let's do this! It's time to RISE!

A Letter to My Readers, My Friends, My Fellow Brothers and Sisters in Christ.

Dear Sweet Friend,

    I want you to know that you are a fierce warrior. Don't let your thoughts or the words of others around you tell you otherwise. You are called to greatness beyond what you can comprehend. You ARE CAPABLE because HE IS CAPABLE. You ARE WORTHY because HE CALLS YOU WORTHY. You are a leader in the life you live. There will be tough hours and days ahead, but you are an overcomer. His promises say that you are bigger than the pain in front of you, and you will laugh in the face of adversity when it's behind you. If you do get to those moments of struggle to see the greatness that's waiting to exude from inside of you, speak life and declare this out loud over yourself and seek His Holy Spirit and His Word:

    I am chosen for greatness.
    I am loved beyond my achievements and despite my flaws.

Through Christ, I am more than my mistakes and stronger than my adversities.

Through Christ, I possess inside of me a power greater than anything I await to face.

I am a beautiful creation.

I am kind, and my words are life-giving.

I am called for a moment greater than now.

I choose to ignore the lies of defeat and act on the truths of victory.

My soul is humble, but my capabilities through Christ are fierce.

I am enough in Him.

I am more than enough in Him.

I am an overcomer, and I WILL overcome with the help of the Holy Spirit.

I will rise above the expected and soar through the winds of magnificence.

I am worthy because my Creator says I am.

Say this out loud over and over until every cell in you is working in accordance with His will. Write this out. Type it out. Print it and recite it daily. Print out Scriptures that the Holy Spirit leads you to as well. When you practice a habit of Scriptural declaration, your life will begin to reflect its truths. You got this sweet friend. Choose to grab hold of your calling to greatness through Jesus Christ.

About the Author

Whitney is a strong-willed, determined, homeschooling mother of three, wife for over 13 years, and multi-tasking extraordinaire. She has been a Registered Nurse by profession for almost ten years and has dedicated years of research to help others in their health journey. Whitney has a heart and passion for loving others and prays daily for the Holy Spirit to use her to help others find who they were created to be in Him. She lives every day trying to bring and represent joy and hope to those who have trouble seeing it. Whitney hopes to leave a legacy as someone who had a servant's heart, who loved people and God wholeheartedly.

www.ingramcontent.com/pod-product-compliance
Lightning Source LLC
Chambersburg PA
CBHW070054110526
44587CB00013BB/1500